THEATRICS IN PATRISTIC PREACHING AND BIBLICAL EXPOSITION

THE CHADWICK-ODEN LECTURES

What can today's Christians learn from voices from the long history of the church in order to understand their faith in a disconnected, digitized, and divided world? This lecture series, supported by Fieldstead and Company (Irvine, California) and hosted by the Premonstratensian (Norbertine) St. Michael's Abbey (Silverado, California), was created in honor of Henry Chadwick and Thomas C. Oden and their leadership among the church and academy. Annual pairs of lectures by leading scholars and authors explore the historical and theological roots of Christianity. They apply ancient, patristic, and early medieval Judeo-Christian thought and expression that approach the faith, not simply as a collection of doctrines, but as a transformative way of life. Videos of the lecture series may be viewed at the website ChadwickOden.org.

1. *Why Does Augustine Matter?* by Rowan Williams (2023)
2. *Why Poetry in the Bible Matters*, by Robert Alter (2024)
3. *Theatrics in Patristic Preaching and Biblical Exposition*, by Paul M. Blowers (2025)

THEATRICS IN PATRISTIC PREACHING AND BIBLICAL EXPOSITION

PAUL M. BLOWERS

Copyright © 2025 by Paul M. Blowers, ICCS Press.

ICCS Press, 616 Prospect Street, New Haven, CT 06511 www.iccspress.com

All rights reserved. No part of this book may be reproduced in any form or by any electronic or mechanical means, including information storage and retrieval systems, without written permission from ICCS Press, except for the use of brief quotations in a book review.

Library of Congress Control Number: 2025941543

Publisher's Cataloging-in-Publication
(Provided by Cassidy Cataloguing Services, Inc.).

Names: Blowers, Paul M., 1955- author. | St. Michael's Abbey (Silverado, Calif.), host institution.
Title: Theatrics in patristic preaching and biblical exposition / Paul M. Blowers.
Description: New Haven, CT : ICCS Press, [2025] | Series: Chadwick-Oden lecture series.
Identifiers: LCCN: 2025941543 | ISBN: 9781624281006 (paperback) | 9781624281013 (Amazon) | 9781624281075 (ePub) | 9781624281020 (Kindle)
Subjects: LCSH: Fathers of the church--Oratory. | John Chrysostom, Saint, -407. | Basil, Saint, Bishop of Caesarea, approximately 329-379. | Romanus, Melodus, Saint, active 6th century. | Preaching--History--Early church, ca. 30-600. | Bible--Homiletical use. | Rhetoric--Religious aspects--Christianity. | Public speaking--Religious aspects--Christianity. | BISAC: RELIGION / Christian Theology / History. | RELIGION / Christianity / History.
Classification: LCC: BV4222 .B56 2025 | DDC: 251--dc23

ISBN: 978-1-62428-100-6 PB; 978-1-62428-101-3 Amazon.

Printed in the United States of America on acid-free paper.

CONTENTS

1. PREACHING THEATRICALLY IN THE
   EARLY CHURCH 1
   Author-Audience Discussion 22

2. PATRISTIC PREACHING ON BIBLICAL
   TRAGEDY 37
   Author-Audience Discussion 59

   Father Hugh's Opening Remarks to the Lectures 73
   Author's Comments and Acknowledgments 75
   Henry Chadwick and Thomas C. Oden 77
   St. Michael's Abbey 79

❆ I ❆
PREACHING THEATRICALLY
IN THE EARLY CHURCH

Introduction: Theatricality in Greco-Roman Culture

A Christian need not look very far in these United States to surmise that we are immersed in a "performance culture": arts and entertainment galore, political theatrics, athletics as a performance culture unto itself, and so on. In all this there is much high drama and suspense amplified by producers, politicians, media pundits, artists and performers, coaches and players, commentators, and by audiences themselves. I presume that you invited me for this lectureship, not simply to learn something new about the early church, but in hopes that I will *perform* well and perhaps say something inspiring and not just informative. If mine is technically an academic lecture, it is still, for better or worse, invariably a piece of styled rhetoric that may or may not have "flair."

Though we are far removed from it historically and contextually, the imperial Greco-Roman culture within which the early Christian movement took root and emerged was itself a kaleidoscopic performance culture, especially though not exclusively favoring spectacle and theatricality, the *feasting of the eyes*. Even though Aristotle, in his *Poetics*, had downplayed spectacle or mere "show" (*opsis* / ὄψις) as essential to an effective plot in staged drama,[1] the Roman poet Horace, during the reign of Augustus, judged that the visual was more potent than the audible in affecting an audience. The "trusty eyes" (*oculi fideles*), says Horace, surpass the ears as vehicles for penetrating people's minds.[2] Horace's younger contemporary the philosopher and playwright Seneca ignored Aristotle and recounted graphic horror in his tragedies lest he not command the eyes of the imagination.[3] These pagan authors flourished in a Roman society teeming with performance spaces and theatricality. Enclosed theaters were not required to accommodate spectacles of all kinds, especially the so-called *ludi*, regular festive "games" or fairs that carried immense cultural and religious significance. In addition to the outdoor circuses used for chariot races and gladiatorial contests, public forums and markets hosted various forms of entertainment, while the porticos of temples staged performances dedicated to their respective gods. Many public spaces could serve as makeshift stages for scheduled or ad hoc celebrations: sacrifices to the gods, divinations, communal prayers, political and military orations, legal trials, executions, marriages, funerals, religious and triumphal parades, even a magistrate's procession through city streets.[4] In addition to dramatized religious rites—there was little in the way of popular religious education in the empire—ritual pageantry, the so-called *pompa deorum*, was vital to promote civic allegiance to the gods.[5]

---

1. *Poetics* 1449b; 1450a; 1453b.
2. *Ars poetica*, ll. 180–82 (Loeb Classical Library 194:464).
3. See esp. Seneca's *Thyestes* (62 A.D.).
4. A. J. Boyle, *An Introduction to Roman Tragedy* (London: Routledge, 2006), p. 3.
5. Jacob Latham, *Performance, Memory, and Processions in Ancient Rome: The* Pompa Circensis *from the Late Republic to Late Antiquity* (Cambridge: Cambridge University Press, 2016), pp. 44–66, esp. 46–49.

We would nonetheless be greatly mistaken to assume that ancient pagans were invariable dupes allured purely by what was eye-catching, or that they were hopelessly addicted to superficiality at the expense of substance—an accusation consistently leveled by early Christian polemicists. The same Roman author, Seneca, who tried to play up bloody spectacle in scripting his tragic plays also understood that sheer visuality would not suffice, that words carried their own power and provocation. There is, in any case, no evidence that Seneca's tragedies were ever actually staged; they were primarily performed as nonstaged readings, and he may even have intended as much since the plays are full of characters' highly stylized rhetorical declamations. In short, *rhetorical performance*—not only in theater but in law, politics, education, and other settings—permeated Roman culture. This trend was reinforced by robust revivals of rhetorical and literary art known as the Second Sophistic (second to third centuries) and later the Third (Byzantine) Sophistic (fifth century), both of which spanned the growth of early Christianity.

That said, across Rome's imperial age, staged drama was gradually declining, and even tragic plays progressively gave way to mimed, sung, danced, or parodied versions of the stories in order to meet entertainment needs. Circus spectacles, however, given the persistent public demand for them, endured well into the post-Constantinian empire and were only slowly suppressed by Christian rulers. The questions we are considering here and which are the subject of a burgeoning scholarship are the following: How, and to what extent, did Christian preachers and authors, as well as liturgists and hymnists, seize the moment to cultivate an effective performance culture of the church's own? Did such a Christian performance culture derive merely from competing with residual paganism? Or did it stem from a conscious and deliberate campaign, on the part of Christianity's own learned protagonists, to bring the scriptures to dramatic life for audiences with very different levels of knowledge of the biblical revelation? And this in an era when, as Augustine among others admitted,[6] the scriptures seemed, by pagan literary and rhetorical standards, to be utterly barbaric and uncouth.

Before I turn more directly to the rise of "theatrical" preaching in the early church, I need to sketch a few key aspects of the formative Christian performance culture that both empowered such preaching and set its standards. One of these, unveiled in the groundbreaking work of Oxford historian Averil Cameron, was the development of what she calls a Christian "rhetoric of empire," seizing on classical paideia, drawing from the riches of pagan literary and rhetorical art, but also generating new modes of discourse that depended on signs and symbols drawn from sacred scripture and that were diffused in an ever more diverse array of Christian texts.[7] Without completely displacing the entrenched religious culture of Rome, Christianity fashioned a new religious language and, just as important, the religious *imagination* to go with it. Furthermore, as another prolific British scholar, Frances Young, has emphasized, Christian leaders and preachers worked to turn the Bible itself into a "classic" (or better yet a canon of classics) rivaling the pagan classics that had long enjoyed cultural dominance.[8] It helped that, early on, brilliant and erudite interpreters and preachers like Origen treated the Bible as an inexhaustible treasury of words, figures, and images nurturing knowledge of the triune God. Augustine, for his part, having compared Scripture with high

---

6. Cf. Augustine, *Confessiones* 6.5.8 (Corpus Christianorum, Series Latina [CCSL] 27:78–79); Arnobius of Sicca, *Adversus nationes* 1.58–59 (Corpus Christianorum Ecclesiasticorum Latinorum [CSEL] 4:39–41).
7. Averil Cameron, *Christianity and the Rhetoric of Empire* (Berkeley: University of California Press, 1996).
8. Frances M. Young, *Biblical Exegesis and the Formation of Christian Culture* (Cambridge: Cambridge University Press, 1997), pp. 47–75; and *Virtuoso Theology: The Bible and Interpretation* (Cleveland: Pilgrim Press, 1990), pp. 26–44.

Ciceronian rhetoric, gloriously and innocently declares that he first approached the Bible as "something neither open to the proud nor laid bare to children; a text lowly to the beginner but, on further reading, of mountainous difficulty and enveloped in mysteries"[9]—for which reason he went on to tackle the Bible's complexity, and to advance its status as a teaching and preaching "classic."[10]

One final, crucial factor in the ferment of a Christian performance culture was the maturing of Christian biblical interpretation itself, as it exploited techniques from pagan literary and rhetorical criticism for exegetical purposes—not just for learned commentators' sake but to inform preaching and liturgy as *live*, "performative" forms of interpretation. Patristic interpreters committed to the excavation of multiple senses of Scripture (literal and nonliteral), and to the principle of Scripture interpreting Scripture, not so much as a matter of strict exegetical method as of urgency to uncover the breadth of revelation and its accommodation to persons of varied levels of maturity and education. It was not enough simply to "prove" the truths of the new Christian revelation using Old Testament testimonies and typologies. "Figural" interpretation, so called, allowed that figures, types, or symbols in the Old Testament might have been fulfilled climactically in Jesus Christ, but the ramifications and iterations of that grand fulfillment were ongoing in the church's foreground and future. Let us recall 1 Corinthians 10:11, so often cited by ancient interpreters, where Paul deduces that various events happened to people in the biblical past τυπικῶς (*typikôs*, "figurally" or perhaps even "mysteriously") for the instruction of us "on whom the end of the ages has come," that is, all those living in the wake

---

9. *Confessiones* 3.5.9 (CCSL 27:31), trans. Henry Chadwick, *Augustine: Confessions* (Oxford: Oxford University Press, 1991), p. 40.
10. E.g., in his influential treatise *De doctrina christiana*.

of Christ's incarnation. This open horizon liberated preachers to ignite the Christian imagination by portraying biblical narratives and characters as playing out an eschatologically oriented drama into which believers in the present were being recruited and engrafted as the latest actors rather than as mere passive observers.

Preaching as Theatrical Performance in Late Ancient Christianity

With this hermeneutical impetus, Christian preaching and liturgy, especially from the fourth century on, became more and more performatively self-conscious, manifest also in the architectural configuration and enhancement of Christian basilicas as performance spaces.[11] Unsurprisingly, most of the extant sermons from the ancient church come from learned and rhetorically well-trained homilists who still saw fit pastorally to calibrate their rhetoric to unlearned or immature audiences. We now have abundant scholarship on the particular rhetorical tools that they deployed to augment and even exaggerate the dramatic impact of the narratives they were expounding. Chief among them was ekphrasis, the redescription of the biblical events and characters with a new vividness (*enargeia / ἐνάργεια*), intended to close the gap between the story and the audience by making the imagery lifelike.[12] Ekphrasis is pervasive in patristic preaching, not only in biblical exposition but in funeral orations, homilies

---

11. For such architectural accommodation of liturgical performance, see Courtney Friesen, *Acting Gods, Playing Heroes, and the Interaction between Judaism, Christianity, and Greek Drama in the Early Common Era* (London: Routledge, 2024), pp. 1–31; Laura Lieber, *Staging the Sacred: Theatricality and Performance in Late Ancient Liturgical Poetry* (New York: Oxford University Press, 2023), pp. 41–55.
12. The best recent analyses of ekphrasis in patristic usage are Lieber, *Staging the Sacred*, pp. 162–229; Ruth Webb, *Ekphrasis, Imagination, and Persuasion in Ancient Rhetorical Theory and Practice* (Abingdon: Routledge, 2009); Morwenna Ludlow,

for martyrs and saints, homilies for special liturgical occasions, and more. Clearly it was vital for enhancing visuality and theatricality. If we compare ekphrastic preaching with theatrical drama, where the proscenium provides the "invisible" or "fourth wall" between the action onstage and the audience, it is as if preachers were actors pressing to the edge of the stage in hopes that their words might puncture the veil to grip and convince the audience. Though there are hundreds of superb examples of ekphrastic preaching on the Bible, I will focus on one that is, in my judgment, exquisitely representative. It comes from Basil of Seleucia, a bishop in southern Asia Minor in the fifth century whose preaching gained wide influence. Imagine, if you will, a basilica packed with people present for the Feast of the Holy Innocents, many of them distracted and unfocused, until Basil mounts his ambo and homes his audience in on Herod's mass infanticide in his hunt for the baby messiah:

> For me, the infants' cries still echo all around, and I have imagined watching them, these babes wailing indiscriminately with terror as they saw the gleaming of the swords and turned in panic to their mothers' arms for safety, then sank into their bosoms. I consider too the mothers themselves looking on, one here and another there passing through the city with their piteous and precious cargo, seeking a place of refuge, and not even receiving a decent veil over their eyes when the danger reached its peak. I think of one mother trying to escape and casting herself into totally unfamiliar courses of action. Still another mother I see vainly flinging her hair over her child, hoping by such modest shelter to steal him away from the

---

Art, Craft, and Theology in Fourth-Century Christian Authors (Oxford: Oxford University Press, 2020), pp. 31–76.

danger. Yet another mother I imagine being violently cornered by her pursuers, then withdrawing, and being stricken with fear and crying her eyes out, and gazing at the flashing sword, dividing her attention between the sword's forward motion and her baby boy about to be hacked, and instinctively insinuating herself between the weapon and the child she holds. In addition, I see another mother able neither to move nor to exhale even a little, frozen in her tracks by terror, having already consumed herself with a parent's proper fear, and awaiting, with faint wailing, the smiting sword.[13]

Remarkably, Basil squeezes all this gut-wrenching detail out of a single verse of Scripture, Matthew 2:16.[14] Its effect was doubtless riveting, reducing the audience, learned and illiterate members alike, to a common lamentation and outrage. Evidence shows that his homily inspired other preachers to intensify the graphic horror of the story of the Holy Innocents in their own homilies. But if the dramatic force of ekphrasis in Basil's sermon seems obvious, I must nevertheless also point out its risks. One of them was the intrinsic difficulty of managing an audience's emotional response. Even if many or most persons were induced to pious grieving over the death of the Holy Innocents, it was altogether possible that others were scared off by the horrific spectacle, or, worse yet, left questioning whether the infant Jesus had escaped the massacre at other babies' expense.

There is a parallel here in the sermons of the fourth-century

---

13. *Oratio* 37.2 (*de infantibus in Bethleem ab Herode sublatis*) (Patrologia Graeca [PG] 85:389c–392a); my translation.
14. "Then Herod, when he saw that he had been tricked by the wise men, was in a furious rage, and he sent and killed all the male children in Bethlehem and in all that region who were two years old or under, according to the time which he had ascertained from the wise men" (RSV).

Cappadocian Fathers on the Christian response to poverty. All three—Basil of Caesarea, Gregory Nazianzen, and Gregory of Nyssa—use ekphrasis to depict the indigent and the diseased in society as public players in a tragedy of epic proportions. The bishops graphically describe the bodily decrepitude of such people, many of them lepers, who unwittingly were actors putting their miseries on full display. In one moving passage, Gregory of Nyssa queries his audience, "Can you see these melancholy dancers, this mournful and wretched chorus? How are they able to parade around with their misfortunes? How are they able to theatricalize their disfigured bodies? How, like jugglers, can they sport their various infirmities before the crowd? They are singers of forlorn melodies, composers of grievous tales, and provide lyrics for their sad compositions. Poets of a new and ill-fated tragedy, they use no alternative tragic themes to evoke emotion, but fill up the stage with their own woes."[15] And yet the more the Cappadocian preachers detailed the bodily maladies of indigent persons in public domains, the more they risked inducing fear in the audience, or nauseating it, or causing indifference rather than evoking compassion and empathy—possibilities all the more plausible because, for centuries, the poor and diseased exposed in Roman society had been far more the objects of disgust and repulsion than of any natural outpouring of pity.[16]

Still another key rhetorical instrument in theatrical preaching, abundantly employed by patristic preachers and poets alike, was prosopopoeia (personification of something or someone not present) and ethopoeia (character development through impersonation). Together they were a stylized attempt to enhance the

---

15. Ibid. (Gregorii Nysseni Opera [GNO] 9/1:116–17).
16. See, on this theme, Susan Wessel, *Passion and Compassion in Early Christianity* (Cambridge: Cambridge University Press, 2016), pp. 65–97.

fuller dimensions of biblical personages and events while seeking to remain thoroughly anchored in the scriptural texts themselves. These techniques could be quite adventurous and carry serious risks, as we shall see.[17] With modern comic impersonators, we are often amazed by their mimicry of the voice and gestures and perhaps the signature phrases of the one they imitate; but they are under no canonical discipline to bring out the latent thoughts, virtues, or vices of their subject. Their role is to exaggerate the persona, not interpret it. In their own art of prosopopoeia and ethopoeia, patristic preachers and poets went much further, crafting monologues on the mouths of biblical characters, and sometimes also creating imagined dialogues between characters. This was not without precedent in the New Testament itself, as when Luke, in the Book of Acts, set forth eloquent speeches on the lips of Peter (Acts 2:14–36; 3:12–26) and Stephen the protomartyr (7:2–53) that were intended to spell out more fully the testimony of their lives and commitments.

A good illustration of this prosopopoeia is a sermon of John Chrysostom on the Rich Man and Lazarus (Luke 16:19–31), where the bishop interposes, in first person, a complaint on the lips of the pauper Lazarus toward his wealthy and luxuriating counterpart:

> Why is this so? This [rich] man living in wickedness and cruelty and inhumanity enjoys all things even beyond his need, and endures no trouble nor any of the unlooked-for reverses that often happen in human affairs. He enjoys unmixed pleasure, while I have not the opportunity of partaking even of necessary food. To this man, who squanders all his substance on parasites and flatterers and wine—to *him* all good things flow like a river; while I live

---

17. For further analysis, see Ludlow, *Art, Craft, and Theology*, pp. 119–43.

as an object to be gazed at—an object of shame and derision, and am wasting away through hunger. Is *this* Providence? Can this be *Justice* that rules over human affairs?[18]

Here Chrysostom creatively quotes Lazarus lamenting his helpless station in life so as to remind his Christian audience of how the impoverished remain objects of scorn and are understandably pressed to question God's justice. No sooner does Chrysostom impersonate Lazarus's complaint, however, than he pulls back, as if recognizing the risk of impropriety in relation to God's own character. Immediately Chrysostom interjects, "[Lazarus] did not say any of these things, nor had he them in his mind. How is this manifest? From the circumstance that guardian angels surrounded him at his death, and bore him away to Abraham's bosom. Had he been a blasphemer, he would not have gained this glory."[19] And yet the cat was out of the hat in John's sermon and he surely knew it. The upshot was a provocative rhetorical tension, allowing the poor to "have their say" about ostensible cosmic injustice while also reassuring his audience that the providence and justice of God are always in command of things.

In this connection, allow me to turn from preaching proper to early Christian hymnody and poetry. Such a move is justified since there was a thin line between homiletics and poetics both in the Syriac Christian *memre*, or verse homilies, and the Byzantine-Christian *kontakia*, or sermonic hymns, all of which had liturgical use. The author par excellence in this regard was the sixth-century hymnist Romanos the Melodist, who, perhaps more effectively and creatively than any of his peers, used

---

18. *Hom. de Lazaro et divite* 1.9 (PG 48:975), trans. F. Allen (London: Longmans, Green, Reader and Dyer; Edinburgh: Ballantyne, 1869), p. 24 (slightly modified).
19. Ibid.

prosopopoeia and ethopoeia in generating a new level of dramatics and theatrics in his various biblical kontakia. We need with these texts always to keep in mind they were a sophisticated form of artistic mimesis. But Romanos, like other Christian poets and preachers, was not out just to imitate the skills of great pagan rhetoricians working to make ancient myths more compelling for a contemporary audience. In Romanos, mimesis is directed toward biblical authors, who are already superior dramatists since they are the stewards of a divine revelation. His theatricalizing of biblical narratives is thus an artistic parallel to the work of exegetes and commentators searching out the so-called *sensus plenior* ("fuller sense") of Scripture as a salvific drama with many hidden plots.

Romanos's kontakia thrive on invented interactions between biblical characters, while he often insinuates his own voice as a narrator presiding over the action and providing theological context. In his kontakion on the Prodigal Son (Luke 15:11–32), for example, he broaches a whole new detail. Instead of the older brother remaining envious when the father invites him to join in the celebration of the return of his prodigal brother, Romanos inserts a happier ending: "When [the elder son] heard [the father's] words, he was persuaded and shared the gladness with his brother. And he began to sing and say, 'All of you, shout with praise, that blessed are they whose every sin is forgiven; and whose iniquity has been covered and wiped away. I bless you, Lover of mankind, who have saved my brother also, you the Master and Lord of the Ages.'"[20] The elder brother's penitent doxology here has no basis in the scriptural text, and could even be seen as violating the story's literal sense, which leaves us repulsed by the brother's presumably unresolved bitterness. But

---

20. *On the Prodigal Son*, strophe 21, trans. Ephrem Lash, *On the Life of Christ: Kontakia* (San Francisco: HarperCollins, 1995), p. 111.

Romanos probably justifies the inference to strengthen the audience's own repentance, or perhaps to inoculate it against the biblically well-attested vice of envy purportedly overcome even by this disgruntled brother. To be sure, it makes for a happier ending.

Less adventurous but more emotionally powerful is Romanos's kontakion on the "sinful woman" who anointed Jesus' feet (Luke 7:36–50). In the story itself she simply acts and never says a word, but Romanos gives her a whole new voice (prososopoeia) and turns her into a paragon of Christian penitence (ethopoeia). Her moving monologues fill up much of the kontakion, intimating her secret musings about approaching the merciful Christ, such that bathing his feet becomes her own baptism:

> I am going to Him for it is for me that He has come. I leave my former friends, for now I earnestly yearn for Him; and I bring perfume to the One who loves me, and I caress him; I weep, I groan, and I try to win Him over to love me. I am changed by my love of the Loved One, and I love my lover as He wishes to be loved. I kneel as I groan, for this He wishes. I am silent and I maintain my silence, for He is delighted with that. I break with the past that I may please the new. In short, I renounce the filth of my deeds.
>
> I shall, then, go to Him, I shall be enlightened, as the Scripture records. I shall draw nigh to God and not feel shame before Him. He does not upbraid me; He does not say, "Hitherto you were in darkness; now you have come to see me, the Sun" [cf. Mal. 4:2, LXX]. Therefore, I take the perfume and go forward. I shall make the house of the Pharisee a baptistery, for there I shall be cleansed of

my sin and purified of my lawlessness. I shall mix the bath with weeping, with oil and with perfume; I shall cleanse myself and escape from the filth of my deeds.[21]

More daring, however, is Romanos's impersonation of Christ himself,[22] including in this same kontakion, where he takes issue with Simon the Pharisee's lack of mercy toward the woman, which is in keeping with what Jesus actually says in the narrative, but goes further in setting Simon and the woman on the same par as debtors to Christ's atoning sacrifice. This seems relatively innocuous, an amplified paraphrase, for which there are many other examples. In the kontakion on the doubting disciple Thomas (John 20:24–29), Romanos develops an extended dialogue between Jesus and Thomas that elaborates how the Savior drew the disciple from doubt to new faith. Supplementing the story as it stands, which implies that Thomas did not have to touch the resurrected Christ's wounds in order to declare him "Lord and God," Romanos has Thomas gradually learning to take ownership of his trust in the Savior.

> [CHRIST:] I slept for a short time in a tomb and after three days came back to life. For you and those like you I lay in a grave, and you, instead of thanksgiving, have brought me unbelief. For I heard what you said to your brothers.
> [NARRATOR:] At this, Thomas trembled and cried out,
> [THOMAS:] "Do not blame me, Saviour, for you I always believe. Peter and the rest I have difficulty in believing,

---

21. *On the Sinful Woman*, strophes 5–6, trans. Marjorie Carpenter, *Kontakia of Romanos, Byzantine Melodist*, I: *On the Person of Christ* (Columbia: University of Missouri Press, 1970), p. 103.
22. On the use of prososopoeia with Christ himself, including its interpretive risks, see Ludlow, *Art, Craft, and Theology*, pp. 144–60.

for I know that they lied to you and, in the hour of evils, they were afraid to say to you, "You are our Lord and God."

[NARRATOR:] He who sees all things, seeing that Thomas was wanting to cast off the offense of unbelief, answered him,

[CHRIST:] You were with them also at the moment to which you referred. For all of you left me to suffer alone....

[. . .]

[THOMAS:] Yes, lover of mankind, I too will perfume you, but not as the harlot did before. I do not approach the myrrh-seller crying, "Give me myrrh." I bring my faith to you who possess grace far above myrrh—the side which I grasp, I enjoy. O Christ, I glorify your faithful condescension; how you became incarnate so that you might deliver, from the vain folly of idols, humanity which you fashioned, and how you accepted, Saviour, being struck so that you might free me from passions, to cry to you, "You are our Lord and our God."[23]

John Chrysostom rather routinely places new speeches on the mouth of Christ (what Jesus *might* have said), although aware of the need to stay within the compass of the scriptural text. In his sermon on the encounter with Nicodemus (John 3:1–15), for example, Chrysostom has Jesus deliver a fuller—and far less patient—exposition of the new birth, couching it in terms of Nicodemus's need to move beyond stubborn fixation with bodily birth and to contemplate something far more ineffable:

---

23. *On Doubting Thomas*, strophes 11–12, 16, trans. Lash, pp. 187–88, 189–90.

I mean another birth, O Nicodemus. Why do you drag down my saying to the earthly? Why do you subject the matter to the necessity of nature? This birth is too high for such pangs as these; it has nothing in common with you; it is indeed called "birth" but in name only does it have anything in common, for in reality it is different. Remove yourself from that which is common and familiar; a different kind of childbirth do I bring into the world; in another manner will I have persons to be generated. I have come to bring a new manner of creation. I formed humanity of earth and water; but that which was formed was unprofitable, since the vessel was wrenched awry. I will no more form them of earth and water, but "of water and the Spirit."[24]

Chrysostom stays relatively close to Jesus' discourse with Nicodemus. In addition, he feels justified to retrofit it with the Church's mature apostolic and patristic teaching on Christ as co-Creator of humanity and on baptism as new creation in a Pauline sense, crediting it directly to Christ himself. Lest water baptism be left out of the mix, John explains how Jesus insinuated water baptism in his announcement of the new birth/creation to Nicodemus.

Not all impersonation of Christ for dramatic effect, however, had to involve putting new words or speeches in his mouth. Ethopoeia allowed the possibility of impersonating Jesus' true emotions and intentions in a given pericope. For example, Basil of Seleucia contends in his homily on the raising of Lazarus that Jesus "wept" (John 11:35) expressly to set limits on Christian grieving: "He wept, he did not lament, or wail, or moan, or rend

---

24. *Hom. in Joannem* 25.1 (PG 59:149); trans. Nicene and Post-Nicene Fathers, 1st series, 14:86 (revised).

his garments, or tear his hair," since such actions are inappropriate for those who hope in resurrection.[25] John Chrysostom takes up the ostensive scandal of Jesus' initial insolence toward the Canaanite woman in Matthew 15, and even second-guesses the disciples' discomfort with the situation, as they are Jesus' other audience besides the woman and an onlooking crowd of other Gentiles. For Chrysostom, the disciples, in telling Jesus that he needs to withdraw from the woman, were hiding their actual, internal sympathy with her desperation. He wants the disciples to save face, but this was hazardous exegetically, since the text clearly portrays the disciples as hardliners needing a lesson in God's universal grace. Chrysostom amplifies the woman's self-awareness of being shameless in imploring Jesus to heal her daughter. He even gives her a new line in the banter: "Though I be a dog, I am not an alien." All the while, Jesus' imperviousness turns out to be a mere ruse, a beneficent ploy both to expose the woman's bold Gentile faith and to publish his generosity to the outsider. Chrysostom recruits Jesus' responses to two other outsiders, the centurion with a paralyzed slave (Matt. 8:5–13), and the Samaritan woman (John 4:18), and applies them here to prove that Jesus was always "in character" in dealing with Gentiles.[26]

The fifth-century bishop Cyril of Alexandria's long *Commentary on John* is teeming with these attempts to fill out Jesus' true emotions and motives. Cyril treats every episode of Christ's ministry as a multifaceted tableau of incarnational grace. There is always more than meets the eye in Christ's urgency to disclose

---

25. Basil of Seleucia, *Hom. in Lazarum* 6, Greek text ed. and trans. Mary Cunningham, "Basil of Seleucia's *Homily on Lazarus*: A New Edition," *Analecta Bollandiana* 104 (1984): 173 (Greek), 180 (trans.).

26. *Hom. in Matthaeum* 52.1–2 (PG 58:517–21). Interestingly, Hilary of Poitiers, among the Latin Fathers, also asserts that the disciples secretly sympathized with the Canaanite woman.

that grace, which for Cyril requires not only providing amplified paraphrase of Jesus' statements but, again, sometimes adding more of what he "intended" to say. In the case of the dramatically confrontational story of the blind man in John 9, with the disciples already provoking Jesus on whether the man was blind from birth because of some ancestral sin, Cyril has Jesus explaining his declaration that this blindness only happened so that the "works of God should be manifest" (9:3):

> It is just as if Jesus had said, in different and simpler language: "The man was not born blind on account of his own sins or the sins of his parents; but since it has happened that he was so affected, it is possible that in him God may be glorified. For when, by power from above, he shall be found free from the affliction which lies upon him and troubles him, who will not admire the Physician? Who will not recognize the power of the Healer shown forth in him?[27] . . . and since I have come to give light to those things that were in want of light, it behooves me to cause light to dwell even in the eyes of the body, if they are diseased with the terrible lack of light, whenever any so afflicted come before me.[28]

For Cyril, Christ's application of a makeshift salve of dirt and spit to the blind man's eyes in turn theatricalized his work, as the original Creator of humanity, to communicate anew, manually and materially, his incarnational grace. And his command to the healed blind man to wash in the pool further pointed to the incarnational grace bestowed through baptismal healing.[29]

---

27. *Comm. in Joannem* 6 (on John 9:3), Greek text ed. P. Pusey (Oxford: Clarendon Press, 1872), 2:151–52, trans. Pusey (London: Walter Smith, 1885), 2:15.
28. Ibid. (on John 9:5) (ed. Pusey, 2:155), trans. Pusey, 2:18.
29. Ibid. (on John 9:6–7) (ed. Pusey, 2:155–59).

Conclusion

In examining these various rhetorical modes—ekphrasis, prosopopoeia, ethopoeia, and so on—used by early Christian preachers, poets, and hymnists to enhance the impact of the biblical narratives, we are wise to acknowledge that not all "theatrical" preaching or communication qualified as theatrical in terms of sheer display or spectacle. Much of the drama of the scriptural revelation, after all, was latent, subtle, and implicit, and seemed, to these ancient interpreters, to demand an art of exposition that would draw an audience into the action and hold them there. Preachers, unlike the writers of hymns and poems, had a clear advantage because, as actors of a sort, they could additionally use voice inflection, timing, bodily gestures, and impromptu rhetorical outreach to their listeners. Hymnists and poets had to depend on written verse, though this limitation also energized them to imbue the language and imagery of their works with dramatic intensity, that could be enhanced also in cantors' performance. Meanwhile, the ritual theatricality intrinsic to liturgy itself was a boon to theatrical preaching. Liturgy already commanded, in principle at least, a "captive" audience as well as canonical traditions and cadences of worship that imposed their own standards on preaching. Indeed, preaching was expected to operate fully in sync with the sequential drama of liturgy rather than to compete with it. Especially from the fourth century on, the ever more elaborate liturgies East and West, from the daily office to the sanctoral cycle to the seasonal celebrations of the Christian year, established the salvation-historical context of Christian worship, setting the larger stage on which the dramas of sacred history could be reperformed in ritual, in sacrament, but also in word. Crucially, the drama of preaching and liturgy worked together to cultivate specific kinds of religious emotions (mercy, sorrow, joy, hope, etc.) that would give fuller experiential texture to faith itself, all the more so as Christians were empowered to recognize these emotions in the biblical saints whose stories they heard in church.

Whether in the context of liturgy, or in the disciplinary contexts of prebaptismal catechesis and postbaptismal spiritual instruction, "theatrical" preaching carried its own kinds of risks. I do *not* think that a primary risk was of falling into competition with the enduring varieties of pagan spectacle. The polemical tradition against Greco-Roman theatrics that began in earnest with early apologists like Minucius Felix and Tertullian, or later ones like Eusebius of Caesarea and the African Lactantius, had secured the conviction among Christian leaders that pagan spectacles operated according to standards entirely foreign to the faith, even if those spectacles apparently allured Christians well beyond the Christianization of the empire.[30]

The greatest risk of theatrical preaching was the intrinsic liabilities of artistic mimesis itself. Long before the Christian era, Plato had castigated the poets and playwrights in Athens for trying to mimic reality, only to sucker the masses with raw emotion and to complicate the task of the philosophers. Such artistic mimesis, he claimed, merely imitated the appearance of what was already only phenomenal, not real.[31] Philosophy alone could gain access to the truth in its own right. Fortunately, Aristotle disagreed and emphasized the potential benefits of artistic

---

30. On the sustained Christian aversion to, and criticism of, pagan theater and spectacle, see Leonardo Lugaresi, *Il teatro di Dio: Il problema degli spettacoli nel cristianesimo antico (II–IV secolo)* (Brescia: Morcelliana, 2008); Heiko Jürgens, *Pompa Diaboli: Die lateinischen Kirchenväter und das antike Theater* (Stuttgart: Kohlhammer, 1972); and Werner Weissman, *Kirche und Schauspiele: Die Schauspiele im Urteil der lateinischen Kirchenväter unter besonderer Berücksichtigung von Augustin* (Würzburg: Augustinus-Verlag, 1972), esp. pp. 25–122.

31. Plato's extended critique of the poets and tragedians appears in *Republic* 601b–612e.

mimesis, whether in a dramatic or rhetorical setting. Christian authors redirected Plato's criticism against pagan theatrics, and embraced Aristotle's rehabilitation of mimesis for their own purposes. The question was whether, for Christian preachers and poets, dramatic mimesis could adequately represent ultimate rather than ephemeral truth.

Certainly there were other risks as well, some of which I have already mentioned, including the potential ostentation of rhetorically second-guessing or "supplementing" Scripture, especially in impersonations of biblical characters or inserting extra details into the Bible's own dramatic plots. Still another risk was that attempting to render the Bible a "classic" might backfire, with the preacher's theatricality drawing attention more to the preacher than to the content of his preaching. Basil of Seleucia, whom I quoted earlier from his sermon on the Holy Innocents, was accused by one early modern critic of rhetorically showing off rather than edifying his audience.[32] Basil of Caesarea mentions the situation, probably self-referential, where the skilled oratory of a preacher brings applause to the point that some in the audience are moved to bitter envy. Basil's close friend Gregory Nazianzen, both a preacher and a poet, muses in his great autobiographical poem,

> But as for me, my aim is to speak the truth
> and I worry whether things are as I say they are, or not.
> For my path leads along a precipice, and to fall from it
> is undoubtedly to fall down to the gates of hell.[33]

---

32. Lenain de Tillemont (France, seventeenth century), as noted by Cunningham, "Basil of Seleucia's *Homily on Lazarus*," p. 162, n. 2.
33. *De vita sua*, ll. 1246–49, ed. and trans. Carolinne White, *Gregory of Nazianzus: Autobiographical Poems* (Cambridge: Cambridge University Press, 1996), pp. 102, 103.

In other words, his eloquent rhetoric might land on theological truth but he sensed he was always a hair's breadth away from falling into deception and taking his audiences down with him. The line between veracity and deceit is perilously thin. Still, Gregory was a master of theatricality and willingly pressed the dramatic imagery of his work to all new levels, confident that, whether expounding Scripture or articulating doctrine, the expansion of Christians' imagination of the dramatic force of divine revelation was indispensable to transforming and elevating their faith.

In my second lecture today, I will be exploring what, in my judgment, was one of the most promising and fertile ventures of dramatic mimesis in early Christianity, namely, the mimesis of tragedy in the interpretation of various biblical narratives, both from the Old and New Testaments. There, I hope to show, the discernment and amplification of tragic features in these stories proved, in preaching and commentary, a crucial complement to traditional theological defenses of divine justice and providence by wedding the experience of tragedy of biblical characters with the lived experience of the Christian faithful.

AUTHOR-AUDIENCE DISCUSSION

AUDIENCE MEMBER: A brilliant lecture and extremely well done. Thank you. As I listened to your presentation, I could not resist—intellectually and philosophically—connecting and contrasting the images of theatricality, poetry, and the art with someone like Martin Luther King Jr. Do you see a connection? All of the key points that you raised can be expressed in an analysis of King and his homiletic strategies and procedures. The letter from the Birmingham Jail, which he also preached as a sermon on the March on Washington, can be thought of in terms of tragedy. All sorts of philosophical questions are raised in the Baptist Church after the four girls are murdered in Birmingham, Alabama.

As I think about your lecture, I am asking myself what would I do with a group of young seminarians or students in black theological institutions to recognize the local, contextual application of this brilliant stuff.

Paul Blowers: Of course, Dr. King was a biblical preacher. He knew these narratives and was aware of what the Exodus narrative meant to the African-American religious traditions. And one of the things I think I would want to connect is the fact that King was acutely aware of the power of his rhetoric and the power to evoke the emotions he wants to evoke. He doesn't just want white people to pity black people; it's got to be something much deeper and more transformative. He knows that a lot of people are fearful of him and fearful of the civil rights movement, generally speaking. You know, he of course was a master at relating the plight of his time to biblical tragedy, and so there is a continuum of this with Christian writers in the early church. We're going to see some of this in the preaching of the Protestant Reformation and its aftermath. Who is more theatrical than George Whitfield, John Wesley's colleague in Oxford, who later on in ministry in England turned out to be a Calvinist against those Arminian Methodists. Whitfield was himself an actor. He was a trained actor. He was cross-eyed. When he spoke, people were compelled, just by that. He was theatrical and demonstrative, but he was also in command. And this is why that last quote from Gregory of Nyssa is so intriguing: "I know how powerful I can sound, but I might just drag everyone to hell if I don't get it right." So it's kind of like you're at that crossroads all the time when you're preaching the word of God. Thank you for your question.

AUDIENCE MEMBER: Thank you very much for this encouraging and inspiring lecture. As you're talking, I'm thinking about two things. One is, of course, the Old Testament. What we've lost is all the sacred drama. We don't have sacred feasts, especially Protestants. We don't have this regular drama or the incense, except on a few occasions. But the theatricality is all there in the Old Testament. And how much of this is built upon? You know, the comment about the prodigal son, the older brother, is beautiful. What if he repented? But every preacher is going to take a risk. One of my seminary professors said, "The first step to heresy is exegesis." That's a good one. So every sermon is a risk. But I guess the other concern is pastors who say, "I want to avoid all theatricality to be safe." Well, now you're boring. That's a different heresy. You're saying God is boring. So, you're at risk no matter what you do.

PAUL BLOWERS: You're absolutely right. I come from a tradition that is not very strong in the appropriation of classical liturgy, and we've congratulated ourselves just on the fact that we recovered weekly communion. That tradition is not something that fed me when I was a young person, and so I've spent my entire life trying to recover some of that discipline. And the advantage, of course, in the liturgical traditions is, as Father Hugh said, the fact that the liturgy is already dramatic. It already provides the bigger context of the economy of salvation into which the preacher is expected to fit and not compete. That's a long-standing problem in nonliturgical traditions: The preaching competes. It takes all the burden of theatricality. So, your points are really well taken. And I resonate with what you're getting at. And you know, to some degree, I think one of the benefits of Tom Oden's work, in particular, is that not only did he point evangelicals to the richness of early Christianity, early Christian religious culture, generally, but to biblical interpretation particularly. He pointed them to the richness of liturgical traditions and the way in which the interpretation of the Bible and the cultivation of liturgy go hand in hand. *That's* a gift to those whom he influenced.

AUDIENCE MEMBER: I just wanted to add a reference to Dr. King. There's an element there which I think is essential in the rhetorical, theatrical context of Christian preaching, and that is the witness of suffering, the witness of the cross, because the cross is the only real drama for us. When the preacher lives it out, even becomes a martyr, then that's the perfect homiletic.

AUDIENCE MEMBER: Thank you for your lecture. Do you see the rise of theatrical homilies as being more or less a direct consequence of the rise of allegorical exegesis around, say, the third century, with Origen and the others at Alexandria?

PAUL BLOWERS: That's a wonderful question. And I think there is a definite correlation. Origen is interesting, because he was a scholar, and then he went to Palestine and was ordained and started preaching, which he hadn't had to do before. So, the rubber starts hitting the road. He has these theoretical outlines of what nonliteral interpretation of Scripture looks like, and he is, of course, famous for his own allegorical interpretation, particularly of Old Testament narratives. But I think that at the end of the day, that helped to induce his own preaching to be more theatrical. Oh, my goodness, his sermons on the Song of Songs are incredibly theatrical. I mean, he calls the Song of Songs basically a dramatic allegory, and this back-and-forth between the Bridegroom, the Logos, and the bride, the soul or collectively the church, is based on a very rich allegorical interpretation of that text. Of course, what Origen would say is that the Song of Songs is "literally" an allegory. So he's kind of free there, you know. One of my favorites that I have my students read is Origen's homily on Noah's ark because there we see his more adventurous allegory. The ark has multiple levels, and the different levels are different levels of spiritual maturity, and so forth. And everything in the ark, everything about the ark, has some sort of spiritual meaning. Even the poop at the bottom of the ark, he says, has meaning. And that's off-putting for a lot of modern readers, obviously, but it becomes a part of the DNA of biblical exposition in an allegorical key.

I think a lot of what I've been talking about ties more into this thing that we now call "*figural* interpretation," as opposed to "figurative interpretation." Figural is the idea that you don't just have a straightforward type in the Old Testament, with a straightforward fulfillment in the New Testament. What if a type may blow open the door? It might be sort of a big bang. Christ doesn't just fulfill many types in the Old Testament. He breaks open unexpected meanings, so that exegesis for Origen and others in his wake is this ongoing heuristic journey to recover meaning. And yes, it's off-putting for my higher-critical biblical colleagues. We talk about and actually debate it a lot, but it's a struggle that many us have had to go through who were trained both in early Christian interpretation and in modern, higher-critical approaches to Scripture.

AUDIENCE MEMBER: I want to relate all this to a contemporary issue. I'm a member of a Presbyterian church, and at one of the recent annual meetings, there was an "Overture," which is like a motion, to sort of declare the book *Jesus Calling* to be heretical. It's a very, very popular devotional book. It's sold millions. It was written by a woman, Sarah Young. She's now passed away. She was a missionary, I believe. The book is written from the standpoint of impersonating Christ talking to you. And so, an overture was made to say it's heretical and, well, a committee was formed. Her husband stood up and defended her. It was all awful and awkward in some sense, too.

My questions: How did the Protestant Reformers view this sort of preaching, this dramatic or theatrical preaching, but also this sort of impersonation of Christ? It's super interesting to hear that these church fathers are doing it somewhat regularly. Related: did the early church fathers encourage the common person to do the same thing?

PAUL BLOWERS: Those are great questions. Often it's believed that the Reformers, generally, just threw the baby out with the bathwater, as far as patristic exegesis was concerned, which is just not really the case. I mean, there were things they didn't like, but I mean, fundamentally, Luther knew that there are things in the Old Testament that are allegorical, that are figurative, things that have to be teased out. His sermon on Jacob wrestling with this being, this divine figure, is a long-standing problem. Who is Jacob actually wrestling with? Those kinds of questions require some interpretive imagination. I'm not so familiar with whether the Reformers pick up on patristic prosopopoeia and ethopoeia. I think there was a sort of built-in constraint in classical Protestant hermeneutics that that would probably caution against anything that might adventure beyond what Luther and Calvin and others said is the literal sense, which they would also insist *is* the true theological sense of the text. Now I don't see any of the authors I'm talking about recommending prosopopoeia as an exercise of devotion, where the people should necessarily be rewriting stories of Jesus, trying to imagine what he might have said. They're operating from a lot of training, knowledge, rhetorical skill, but it's still adventurous at times. That's why it's so fascinating to me; how you can just be right on the edge of pushing beyond. It's like this story of the Prodigal Son's brother: if he's penitent, the whole story changes. The tragedy is the brothers left hanging. And we're going to see that this afternoon. The way some preachers don't like stories that get left hanging. They don't like existential dead-ends. We'll see how some of that works out. The writers I am talking about are acutely aware that they are under not only biblical constraints, but they are under their own rhetorical constraints. The Cappadocians are especially aware of this. As I said, Gregory Nazianzen is on this. He's maybe the most brilliant orator in the early church, but he knows he can sink his own ship really fast. But the adventurousness is thrilling. And how are you going to search for the *sensus plenior*, the fuller sense of Scripture, which is endorsed from the early church through the Middle Ages and beyond? Are you going to do that without adventuring to some degree? And so I find all this so intriguing. I'm happy to see that these writers were at least willing to take some risks. I have no doubt, by the way, that some of these people were criticized by their peers. My goodness, the Cappadocian Fathers—the three of them—can rail at each other. And they're all acutely aware of the dangers of rhetoric. Gregory Nazianzen virtually crucifies Gregory of Nyssa for thinking about becoming a teacher of rhetoric instead of becoming a priest. So these folks know what they're up against.

The other thing that fascinates me is that they understand there are a lot of people out there who are not literate in the Bible and who could easily be duped. I always tell my students, remember, these folks didn't have Bibles in their homes. They didn't have multiple translations. Most of what they know they've heard in church, they've heard in the liturgy. We are a long way from the privatization of biblical reading. So, yes, this is really important territory. I think these folks are always aware that they're catechizing. They're always trying to help people understand their biblical faith in the light of their baptism and the full ramifications of it, and they want the Bible to be hard. I mean, Origen knows the Bible's hard. Augustine knows the Bible's hard. They want it to be hard. They want it to be scandalous. You know, it is scandalous, and it's OK to tease the scandal out a little more, but it's always a risk, you see, without having the Bible say something that it is not saying? So this is all good stuff for modern preachers to consider. I think there's a lot to be learned in contemporary homiletics.

AUDIENCE MEMBER: Thank you so much for the talk. So, my understanding was that there was at least a time in the early church where the church didn't just condemn the pagan excesses or corruptions in the theater, but theater in general: actors on a stage talking to each other, interacting, acting out the action. So, it's really fascinating to me to hear that there was maybe even at the same time this theatricality in preaching. I'm tempted to compare it to Plato condemning theater while also writing his philosophy in dialogues. It feels inconsistent. So, I'm curious of two questions. One is a historical timeline question: am I right that there was a time where the church was both doing this theatrical thing with preaching and condemning theater proper? And the second question is: if I'm right, that it happened as inconsistent or in tension with each other, do you see a way that these fit together?

PAUL BLOWERS: You've, in some ways, answered your own question. I mean, very early on, the condemnation of pagan theater in all of its forms is constant. Every kind of visual entertainment in the Roman culture is seductive and dangerous. That can be everything from gladiatorial conflicts and chariot races all the way to the most astute forms of tragedy and comedy. It's all visual seduction. It's all fake at the same time. And they're kind of siding with Plato's critique, but at the same time they're paying attention to Aristotle's tradition through his poetics and rhetoric: that the Bible is profoundly dramatic, and it is evoking dramatic kinds of emotions. And so I'd say theatrical preaching is going on pretty early. By the fourth century particularly, and as Christianity is becoming more comfortable in its Roman skin, not fearing persecution, feeling like certain cultural battles are at least partially being won, fewer people are going to the theater, although they are still Christians going to the theater. There's more of a sense of liberation on the part of Christian rhetoricians to be theatrical. And this stuff is everywhere. I mean, it's in letters. It's not just in sermons and poems and hymns, and so on. And again, my take on it is these people see the scriptures as intrinsically dramatic. If we use some insights from the pagan traditions and other playwrights, so be it. You'll get Christian authors who will occasionally—even Lactantius, who was an apologist in the early fourth century who absolutely vilifies just about everything about the Roman Empire—quote a line from Euripides, and has a famous line where he says, not every poetic work is totally false, sometimes they have hidden truths. That's kind of his concession at the end of the day that some of this stuff is very powerful. And even Plato knew this. In the *Republic* where he quotes this Athenian legislator telling the tragedians, look, we have the true tragedy. Our understanding of the *Republic* is the best tragedy because it explains the best form of human *politeia*, or organization amid all the strains and stresses of life. Plato knows he can't completely trash the tragedians. And Aristotle really departs from Plato on that whole thing.

AUDIENCE MEMBER: Every story, whether it's fictional or biblical, is kind of like an iceberg where you have the tip of the story and then all kinds of underlying things. You're just getting a glimpse of what's going on. And part of dramatizing a text is to hypothesize what's underneath that tip of the iceberg. Judith Weston wrote a very famous book, *Directing Actors*. And in there she has a chapter on interpretation of the script. It's very interesting. She has a rule of three, where she says that you have to, for example, hypothesize, "What is this character's deeper, subconscious, perhaps life, global need, or in this particular text, what is this character's particular agenda?" So, for example, if applying it to Scripture—she doesn't do this—consider Judas and you could say Judas viewed Jesus as dangerous. Or you could say Judas was envious of Jesus. That's another completely different take. And then she says, you want to have one that's the opposite. So, you could say that Judas was trying to force Jesus' hand, to provoke him to act . . .

PAUL BLOWERS: You're jumping on to one of my points this afternoon! You're absolutely right. Very fascinating. In theater, ethopoeia happens on stage. Character development happens on stage. You can have a script, and two actors will play the same character very differently. They'll take it in very different ways, because they're trying to get into their psyche, and they're trying to see how this character fits into the larger plot. And there's a lot of room for creativity, and that's why live theater is so much better than a lot of movie stuff. But anyway, you're right, it's what we're going to see this afternoon, when trying to read some of these problematic characters, particularly in the Old Testament, but also in the New Testament. How do you take them? The question will be posed with Judas. Is he a born loser, or is he somebody that was capable of penitence, a grand model of the penitent life until maybe the very end of his life.

AUDIENCE MEMBER: This was a riveting lecture. I learned a lot. I actually had very little knowledge of this ancient tradition of fleshing out these biblical stories. I have a question concerning hagiographies, early ones, but which I don't have too much knowledge about. I'm more familiar with the medieval and the Baroque-era hagiographies, which, regardless of how fantastical they may seem, I personally feel inclined to believe, just because I see so much spiritual merit in them. And I'm wondering if the people that wrote those meant those to be taken literally, or were they just merely hyperbolic to get people to sort of feel moved. It is really eye-opening to me that what you're telling me about these sermons and these homilies, that it sounds like they're maybe not really meant to be taken literally. My extension of this question is that there seems to be a literalist backlash against taking these hagiographies and venerable stories about the lives of our Lord and the Blessed Mother literally during the Reformation, during the Enlightenment, and as recently as the liturgical renewal of the 1960s where there's so many venerable old stories of saints in the sacral that were just done away with, because I guess there wasn't proof behind them.

And so, I'm asking you, were these intended to be taken literally, or were they intended to be taken just as moral stories? Or are they just made up? Thank you.

PAUL BLOWERS: That is a loaded question. I guess I would have to just come down to the basics that you know. I've done some work in hagiography, yet have not made a career out of it, but I have some friends that work a lot in it. And I think you can't take them all together as being all very much on the same agenda. There are hagiographical pieces where it's very clear that the author is aware that some of this stuff may sound a little unbelievable. John Moschus, who wrote this work in antiquity called *The Spiritual Meadow*, seems to be aware that there may be some skepticism out there. Theodoret of Cyrrhus and his history of the monks in Syria seems to be aware that that some hagiographical kind of narrative could sort of take on a life of its own, that it becomes too adventurous. But the very nature of hagiography is to amplify, right? I mean, there are canons within hagiography. A lot of early hagiographers are trying to match how such and such a saint looks like Jesus, looks like one of the other biblical saints. And so, there are disciplines being built into the tradition, a kind of commonsense tradition of hagiography. Again, there are some which are fairly embellished. I don't think you can deny that they have very extravagant kinds of imagery and rhetoric attached to them, but I don't know that it's necessarily important for us, when we read the hagiographies, to be just concerned about what is absolutely according to historical fact and what is being developed by the hagiographer. These texts became popular literature. These texts also become vehicles of biblical interpretation. And so they play a vital role. And, oh my gosh, prosopopoeia happens all over the place in hagiography, and where you're using ethopoeia, where you're developing the character. You're trying to see what's going on in their mind as they experience events and so on. So I don't have a straightforward answer to your question, other than to say that I would steer people away from being all consumed about what should be taken literally and what is fabricated.

AUDIENCE MEMBER: So, I have two questions pulling on two different threads. The first one has to do with this: when I was listening to your presentation, I was thinking, what you're really talking about are good, strong, classic elements of storytelling, no matter what form you're using, these different strong elements of storytelling, which of course, if you are preaching, you want to reach both the mind and the heart of the people you're speaking to. And so some of this sort of artistic license or storytelling within there, some of the examples you gave made me think, well, we need to consider the context in which that story was being told. Perhaps they knew something about their audience. Perhaps they thought this will touch their hearts, which will bring them, you know, further into the church. So, I'm wondering if you found that in your in your research and history, whether you could say yes, that would be one of the things that people were considering. And my second question has to do with your first slide, and you may talk about it this afternoon, so maybe I'm jumping ahead, but the first slide I thought about you were saying, well, there's some importing of the secular culture, of the culture in which the audience they're speaking to also might exist. So the Roman culture and spectacle and things like that being considered in the presentations in church. I'm wondering whether you think there are new methods of storytelling or new aspects of culture that are being imported into preaching now.

Paul Blowers: On your first question, I think you're right about storytelling. And for example, with this passage I was talking about, where the Prodigal Son's brother is turned into a kind of heroic figure at the end, well, what's going on there is the attempt by the preacher to really pay attention to how this is being registered in the audience. He feels nervous about leaving them with a bad taste in their mouth. And also, remember, folks, I mean this, there's a basic human identification with the older brother. He feels ripped off, he doesn't know what to do. Have you all seen the famous Rembrandt of the Prodigal Son? Absolutely stunning. And the elder brother is just this creepy figure in the background. But, I mean, he's a compelling figure, so the preacher wants to turn him into a hero. Well, it's not true to the story. That's one of those where you may be pushing it too far. Now, your other point. Let's face it, preachers do what politicians do. They try to read the cultural moment, don't they? and capitalize on it and some do it better than others, I suppose, but contextualization of the gospel in any culture is hard, hard business. I've had several friends who were longtime missionaries in Kenya. One of my closest friends was a missionary among the Maasai people in Kenya for about twenty years, and he said, you can learn the Maasai language, and you can speak it with Maasai people, and they're very appreciative of the fact that you've learned their language. But their language—getting a handle on the idioms of their culture, let alone on their language—is like, oh my goodness. I think the difficulty for contemporary preachers now is just trying to manage the way in which our culture has so saturated people, saturated them with imagery. You can't even talk about cars without cars being all about performance. The driving experience needs to be an aesthetic experience, not just a kinetic experience. You don't need to be just moved. You need to be taken out. You're taken out into some glorious place, all by yourself with gorgeous views, and the car has every possible accoutrement in it. We have to navigate a culture in which there's so many bids out there for our attention; that, in itself, was an ascetical discipline for preachers. And let's face it, we see all kinds of overreach in all Christian traditions, in preaching. Homiletics is such an important field right now.

❧ 2 ❧
PATRISTIC PREACHING ON BIBLICAL TRAGEDY

Naïveté about the character of God's self-revelation in Scripture is by no means a purely modern or Western problem. Such naïveté, in the history of interpretation, has cut different ways. One version of it, of which early Christian interpreters were already cognizant, was the overly pious assumption that Scripture would never represent the just and provident God in a negative or problematic light. When Origen, the greatest biblical scholar of the early Christian era, left his native Alexandria for Caesarea of Palestine in the early third century, and was ordained to the priesthood and started preaching, he was able to put to practical use his deep reflections on the nature of Scripture from earlier in his career. His influential treatise on Scripture and interpretation in book IV of his treatise *On First Principles* gave considerable attention to what he called *skandala*, "stumbling blocks" wisely implanted in the biblical text by the Holy Spirit to prompt readers to search for a deeper meaning befitting the integrity of God's revelation. Such *skandala*, Origen suggests, come in many forms: for example, inconsistencies in the sacred history so egregious that they evoke falsehoods; grossly anthropomorphic images of God; utterly bizarre laws in the Pentateuch; "hard sayings," such as Jesus' brusque statement to the Canaanite woman, "I was sent only to the lost sheep of the house of Israel" (Matt. 15:24).[1] I think we are justified to add to the list of *skandala* those narratives and characters in the Bible from which the interpreter is agonizingly challenged to squeeze any redeemable meaning. Origen certainly recognized these. One of them, which we will be exploring shortly, is the seemingly senseless sacrificial death of the daughter of the Israelite mercenary Jephthah (Judg. 11).

Recognizing Tragedy in the Bible

The Jephthah story was one among others in Old and New Testaments that certain early Christian preachers and commentators treated as biblical *tragedies*, opening the door mimetically and theatrically to amplify the tragic dimensions of these narratives and even to draw upon pagan sources regarding the nature of tragedy on stage and in real life. In earlier work that I have done on this subject, I have proposed that the key reason that Greek and Roman tragedy remained a resource for Christian as well as pagan authors was that it had already undergone a long tradition, not only of philosophical critique and filtering, but also of constructive reworking.[2] Plato's rebuke of the tragedians, as I mentioned in my first lecture, had hardly been the final word on the value of tragedy as a literary and dramatic genre. How could it be, when the tragedies of Sophocles, Euripides,

---

1. Origen, *De principiis* 4.2.7–4.3.15, Greek text ed. and trans. by John Behre, Oxford Early Christian Texts (Oxford: Oxford University Press, 2017), pp. 508–60. Bible quotations are from the RSV.
2. See Paul M. Blowers, *Visions and Faces of the Tragic: The Mimesis of Tragedy and the Folly of Salvation in Early Christian Literature* (Oxford: Oxford University Press, 2020), pp. 12–20.

Aeschylus, and others were so replete with timeless themes relating to divinity, providence, evil, suffering, human freedom, and destiny? Seneca, as a Stoic, desired to compose tragedy precisely for its *philosophical* benefits.³ To be sure, Christian polemicists like Tertullian smeared Greco-Roman tragedy, having degenerated into danced and mimed versions, as just another medium of the visual seduction typical of pagan entertainment culture.⁴ Later Christian authors like Eusebius of Caesarea conceded that in the history of Greco-Roman civilization the authors of tragedy, no matter their vices, had qualified as theologians of a sort, propagating mythic dramas that had informed pagan culture for centuries.⁵ Eusebius, and Clement of Alexandria long before him, recognized that Christianity would ignore the tragedians to its own peril. Even if awkwardly or accidentally, the tragedians sometimes landed on truths of great consequence, or at least ignited reflection on the character, dispositions, and activities of God and the gods.

All the while, Aristotle's valorization of tragedy, and of the effectiveness of its plots to transform audiences, provided additional incentive to Christian homilists and interpreters as they explicated the unique features of biblical tragedies. Among the elements of effective tragic plots, Aristotle had included the need for "probability or necessity," indicating a realism and appropriate complexity more likely to grip an audience. Other elements included larger-than-life characters who were still, like us, morally mutable; the occurrence of a protagonist's *hamartia* (ἁμαρτία), less a latent tragic flaw per se than a horrific miscalculation; and the character's recognition (*anagnôrisis* / ἀναγνώρισις) of its consequence, namely, a precipitous reversal of fortune

---

3. On this point, see esp. Gregory Staley, *Seneca and the Idea of Tragedy* (New York: Oxford University Press, 2010).
4. *De spectaculis* 23 (Corpus Christianorum, Series Latina [CCSL] 1:247).
5. *Praeparatio evangelica* 4.1.2 (Sources Chrétiennes [SC] 262:70).

(*peripeteia* / περιπέτεια). In addition, all the tragic pathos aimed, as Aristotle argues, at the catharsis of an audience's own emotions of fear and pity.[6]

Clearly there was much to work with here in eliciting tragic characters and themes in biblical stories, but for patristic interpreters, the goal was not to adhere strictly to Aristotle's expectations but to honor biblical authors themselves as prolific tragedians on their own terms. That said, I will be speaking here not simply of terribly sad stories in the Bible, but of those that raised or implied serious questions of humanity's ultimate stability vis-à-vis divine providence.

Tragedy in the Old Testament

Many patristic preachers and poets had to look no further than the primeval history in Genesis to find the makings of severe tragedy. The story of "the Fall" in Genesis 3 unsurprisingly elicited substantial commentary in early Judaism and Christianity alike, much of it aimed at filling gaps or spelling out implications of the narrative. For post-apostolic Christian interpreters, elements of classical tragedy were unmistakable in Eden: the lead characters' grievous miscalculation (Aristotle's word for it, *hamartia*, is the go-to word for "sin" in the Septuagint and New Testament) (Gen. 3:1–6); their sudden recognition of their trespass in the experience of nakedness (3:7–13); their pathos-laden expulsion from paradise (3:14–24). There was no question of impugning the Creator, in which case interpreters had to explore what possibly could lead creatures dwelling in optimal circumstances in God's presence to bring ruination on themselves. Inevitably this meant identifying the particular vice that induced the transgression, seemingly a tragic flaw waiting to

---

6. *Poetics* 1450b, 1451, 1452a, 1452b, 1453a.

become overt, for which the creature alone was responsible. Since many patristic interpreters treated Adam and Eve as protoascetics being tested from the outset of their existence, identifying this vice was all the more relevant. For Basil of Caesarea, inspired by Origen, the vice was satiety or overindulgence in the goods of creation, resulting in "indecisiveness" (*aboulia/ἀβουλία*).[7] For John Chrysostom it was sloth (*rhathymia / ῥαθυμία*) pure and simple, indolence in embracing virtue.[8] For Gregory of Nyssa it was envy (*phthonos / φθόνος*),[9] as modeled by the Devil himself (Wisd. 2:24). For Augustine, famously, it was pride (*superbia*),[10] while for Maximus the Confessor it was narcissistic self-love (*philautia / φιλαυτία*).[11] Such thinking had the advantage of portraying human vice in the concrete rather than the abstract, and of tracking its tragic legacy as a mimetic domino effect, a tragedy continuing to unfold among all of Adam's descendants.

For other interpreters, like Ambrose of Milan, Augustine, and the lesser-known episcopal poet Avitus of Vienne, the Fall was something more like a tragic comedy of fateful errors, a series of disastrous miscues between the characters of the Serpent, Eve, and Adam. After Adam's original and intimate communing with God, Satan's deception of Eve (the woman becoming Satan's agent) undermined communication between Eve and Adam over God's directive about partaking of the trees of paradise (Gen. 2:16-17), which in turn upset the normative

---

7. *Homilia: Quod Deus non est auctor malorum* 7 (Patrologia Graeca [PG] 31:344d-345a).
8. *Hom. in Genesim* 14.2, 4 (PG 53:114, 116); ibid. 16.4 (PG 53:130); *Hom. adversus eos qui dicunt daemones gubernare res humanas* 1.3; 3.5 (PG 49:249, 262).
9. Gregory of Nyssa, *De vita Moysis* 2 (Gregorii Nysseni Opera [GNO] 7/1:122); cf. *Oratio funebris in Meletium episcopum* (GNO 9:446).
10. *De Genesi ad litteram* 11.5.7 (Corpus Scriptorum Ecclesiasticorum Latinorum [CSEL] 28/1:338-39); *De civitate Dei* 14.11 (CCSL 48:432).
11. *Capita de caritate* 2.8, ed. Aldo Ceresa-Gastaldo, *Massimo confessore: Capitoli sulla carità* (Rome: Editrice Studium, 1963), p. 92; ibid. 3.7 (p. 146); ibid. 3.56-57 (p. 170); also *Ep*. 2 (PG 91:397a-b).

hierarchy of communication between God, man, and woman. Deception thereupon became endemic in human language itself, with the only future hope being the church to restore true hierarchy and cleanse human language.[12] In his recasting of Genesis 2 and 3 as a tragedy, Avitus uses prosopopoeia to place new rhetorical declamations on the lips of Satan (the Serpent), Eve, and Adam, and here we see some of the same risks as I described in my first lecture. Avitus of Vienne has Satan sounding like a spiritual director, seducing Eve and Adam with heavenly knowledge as an altogether worthy attainment. And Eve in her turn seduces Adam with what she calls her newfound wisdom. Satan thus fallaciously jump-starts the human pursuit of a higher contemplation of things, tricking Adam and Eve into seeking a knowledge for which they are not at all prepared or capacitated.[13]

Meanwhile, most preachers and commentators were not satisfied with making Satan the fall guy in the story (pardon the pun). There was, after all, the unfortunate matter of the guilt and shame and its deeper source, since these seem to be not a mere consequence of the sin but the function of an antecedent and altogether fateful failure. Was the freedom of Adam and Eve a blessing or a curse, the cause of a creaturely unraveling? I find two principal trajectories in patristic interpretation here. One, predominantly in the East, imagined a specific kind of ignorance in Adam and Eve—not an innocent mistakenness but a *willful* self-delusion, or in Gregory of Nyssa's view, the "invention" of a

---

12. Cf. Ambrose, *De paradiso* 12.52–56 (CSEL 32/1:309–16); Augustine, *De Genesi ad litteram* 11.30.39; 11.34.45 (CSEL 28/1:362–64); ibid. 11.31.41 (pp. 364–65). For analysis, see also Eric Jager, *The Tempter's Voice: Language and the Fall in Medieval Literature* (Ithaca, NY: Cornell University Press, 1993), pp. 23–98.
13. See George Shea's translation of Avitus's epic poem *On Original Sin*, in *The Poems of Alcimus Ecdicius Avitus* (Tempe, AZ: Medieval and Renaissance Texts and Studies, 1997), pp. 80–89.

totally illusory good,[14] since, in principle, one could not truly see the divine good and not desire it at the exclusion of everything else. The couple was not just conned or fooled; it "knew" and pursued an evil masquerading as a good, and since, as Athanasius, the Cappadocian Fathers, and other theologians claimed, moral evil has no "being," no metaphysical status in creation, and is wholly an existential illusion, the sin in paradise was like a reversal in the direction of nonexistence and oblivion—the cosmic tragedy of tragedies.[15] Ultimately this view was not entirely satisfactory to Augustine and to the interpretive trajectory he generated in the Western church, carrying still too much the sense of mere negligence. Augustine insisted that Adam and Eve looked upon evil as evil and chose it anyhow, wreaking a fateful *necessitas* on themselves and their progeny by devastating true freedom as enjoyed solely by grace.[16]

And yet, for many early Christian preachers and poets, biblical tragedy seemed to take on a whole new bitterness, anguish, and fatefulness in "chapter 2" of the Fall: the story of Cain and Abel (Gen. 4). Though still part of primeval history, now saw human civilization past Eden took concrete shape, including religious worship. No longer was Satan directly intruding; rather, evil appeared surreptitiously like an animal "crouching at the door" (Gen. 4:7) and waiting to pounce. The difficulty here was the appearance that God may have set Cain up for his failed sacrifice. Unlike his father, Adam, who was forewarned by the Creator about eating of the trees in Eden (Gen. 2:16-17), Cain was admonished by God about his inferior harvest

---

14. *De virginitate* 12 (GNO 8.1:298-99); cf. already Athanasius, *Contra gentes* 7, ed. Robert Thomson (Oxford: Oxford University Press, 1971), p. 18; *De incarnatione* 5 (Thomson, p. 146).
15. See esp. Athanasius, *De incarnatione* 4 (SC 199:276-78).
16. Cf. *De perfectione justitiae hominis* 2.2 (CSEL 42:4-5); *De natura et gratia* 66.79 (CSEL 60:293).

offering only *after the fact* (Gen. 4:7); and *only* in the Septuagint and Old Latin versions is a reason given for its failure: that Cain did not "rightly divide" his sacrifice. To avoid an unseemly determinism, some patristic interpreters pointed to verse 3 of the narrative, where it says that only "after some days" did Cain offer his sacrifice, inferring that he had kept back some of the first fruits from God.[17] Be that as it may, they focused not on Cain's greed but on his self-destruction through envy of Abel, whose sacrifice God accepted. Envy and other invidious passions had a profound history in Greco-Roman tragedy and moral philosophy alike, so it is no surprise that various early Christian sermons and treatises made a virtual science of envy and jealousy and their potentially deadly results.[18] More even than the story of Adam and Eve, the narrative of Cain's murder of Abel posed an *ontological* question about the origins of human evil. The text could be read such that Cain *was* vile rather than that he *became* vile. His subsequent chastisement echoes God's original punishment of Adam's disobedience by the cursing of the ground itself (Gen. 3:17); now, with Cain, the ground is doubly cursed because it holds the blood of the innocent Abel. In one early Christian version of the apocryphal *Life of Adam and Eve*, Cain tries to bury Abel in the ground, but his bones keep protruding from the grave because the ground refuses to abide his murdered body.[19] The material creation rises up in indignation against human infection. Though ultimately protected by God, Cain's exile as a fugitive "away from the presence of the Lord," "east of Eden"

---

17. See, e.g., John Chrysostom, *Hom. in Genesim* 18.4–5 (PG 53:154–55); Ephrem the Syrian, *Comm. in Genesim* 3.2 (Corpus Scriptorum Christianorum Orientalium 152:47–48).

18. For analysis, see Paul M. Blowers, "Envy's Narrative Scripts: Cyprian, Basil, and the Monastic Sages on the Anatomy and Cure of the Invidious Emotions," *Modern Theology* 25 (2009): 21–43.

19. *Book of Adam* 40.3–5a, trans. Jan-Pierre Mahé online: https://www2.iath.virginia.edu/anderson/vita/english/vita.geo.html.

(Gen. 4:15–16), has more the look of a tragic fatalism than just an episode of moral estrangement. This seeming existential dead-end inspired more hopeful responses, such as one anonymous Syriac poet who again turned to prososopoeia, penning a beautiful dialogue in which the Christ-figure Abel counsels and consoles Cain about the ramification of his murder.[20] John Chrysostom goes so far as to say that the exiled Cain, while suffering a tremor (cf. Gen. 4:12, 14, LXX: "groaning and trembling on the earth"), lived happily ever after displaying to others the penalty for sin and the need for repentance.[21]

In the Old Testament, however, few narratives could compete for sheer horror and tragic pathos with that of Jephthah and his fatal vow to God in Judges 11. Patristic homilists and other interpreters struggled to make any theological sense of it. Here, after all, was a judge in Israel (Judg. 12:7), on whom the "Spirit of the Lord" had landed (11:29), and who later found a place in the litany of biblical saints recorded in Hebrews 11. Lending himself to his native Gileadites as a mercenary in their conflict with the Ammonites, Jephthah swore a vow that, if God granted him victory, he would sacrifice the first thing to come out of his house at the victory celebration. When it was his daughter who appeared, he anguished that he could not reverse his vow, with the daughter honorably submitting to become a burnt offering after being allowed to mourn her virginity with her companions.

Here was an extreme challenge to squeeze novel nuances and implications from an ostensibly irredeemable story. Some expla-

---

20. *Sōghīthā (Poetic Dialogue) on Cain and Abel*, Syriac text, ed. and trans. Sebastian Brock, "Two Syriac Dialogue Poems on Abel and Cain," *Le Muséon* 113 (2000): 333–75; English trans. reprinted in Sebastian Brock, *Treasure-House of Mysteries: Explorations of the Sacred Text through Poetry in the Syriac Tradition*, Popular Patristics Series 45 (Yonkers, NY: St. Vladimir's Seminary Press, 2012), pp. 51–60.
21. *Hom. adversus Judaeos [against Judaizing Christians]* 8.2 (PG 48:930).

nations were more adventurous than others, since Jephthah needed to be made out a tragic hero rather than a villain. Responses in Christian preaching and commentary ran a wide gamut. John Chrysostom saw the story as a preemptive strike against idle vows to God.[22] Ephrem the Syrian extolled Jephthah for his exemplary grieving and stoic courage at his daughter's demise.[23] Ambrose conceded Jephthah's tragic character as the victim of a *miserabilis necessitas*.[24] Jacob of Sarug, a Syrian preacher, insisted that Jephthah intentionally sacrificed his daughter to prefigure the divine Father's sacrifice of his beloved Son.[25] Augustine allowed that Jephthah, even if unwittingly, was a Christ figure who sacrificed his child in the manner that Christ sacrifices his child the church.[26] Various other authors chose to focus on the ascetical virtue of Jephthah's daughter, who submitted to her father's vow and engaged in godly lamentation of her imminent death.

Elsewhere, patristic preachers were thoroughly familiar that just as kings had been major subjects in Greco-Roman tragedy, so too the Bible had its own beleaguered royalty, who, like the judge Jephthah, were the cause of their own undoing. Some modern Old Testament scholars consider King Saul's demise as the closest narrative to Greek tragedy in all of Hebrew Scripture.[27] For ancient interpreters, however, there was the

---

22. *Hom. de statuis* 14.3 (PG 49:147).
23. See Maria Doerfler's analysis of Ephrem's interpretation in her *Jephthah's Daughter, Sarah's Son: The Death of Children in Late Antiquity* (Berkeley: University of California Press, 2019), pp. 107–8.
24. *De officiis* 3.12.78, Latin text ed. and trans. Ivor Davidson (Oxford: Oxford University Press, 2002), 1:402.
25. *Hom. on Jephthah's Daughter*, ll. 15–18, 58, 61–66; Syriac text with translation by Susan Ashbrook Harvey and Ophir Münz-Manor (Piscataway, NJ: Georgias Press, 2010), pp. 10, 11, 16, 17.
26. *Quaestiones in Heptateuchum* 7.49.26 (CCSL 33:372).
27. Cf. J. Cheryl Exum, *Tragedy and Biblical Narrative: Arrows of the Almighty* (Cambridge: Cambridge University Press, 1992), pp. 16–44; Klaus-Peter Adam, "Saul as

disturbing fact that God had approved and advanced Saul's kingship only later to regret it (1 Sam. 15:11). Like Jephthah, the "Spirit of the Lord" visited him (10:10; 11:6), but later it was displaced by an "evil spirit" (16:14) that left and returned depending on Saul's behavior. Did Saul freely ruin his kingship? Or was he a tragic pawn in the larger scheme of God's dealings with Israel, at last pressed to the breaking point by God's favor for David? Was Saul predestined merely to be an object lesson? The very fact that early interpreters like Origen and Tertullian dismissed outright the possibility that God, rather than Saul himself, was responsible for the king's downfall, indicates a prior perception of the story's potential scandal.[28] It helped that patristic interpreters could target the seemingly unmistakable tragic flaw of Saul, the envy and malevolent jealousy that were manifest in his stormy relation to David. Cyprian of Carthage and Basil of Caesarea profiled Saul's envy in a trajectory with that of Cain.[29] In three homilies on Saul and David, John Chrysostom studied the anatomy of his envy as a deadly combination of fury (orgê / ὀργή), a jealous "leer" (hypopsia / ὑποψία), and invidious malice (baskania / βασκανία).[30] Most drastically, Saul's envy was directed precisely against his own benefactor David, such that David's upward spiral into virtue became commensurate with Saul's downward spiral into vice. And yet, in his characteristic resistance to allowing existential dead-ends in the Bible

---

a Tragic Hero: Greek Drama and Its Influence on Hebrew Scripture in 1 Samuel 14, 24–46 (10,8; 13,7–13a; 10,17–27)," in *For and Against David: Story and History in the Books of Samuel*, ed. Erik Eynikel and A. Graeme Auld (Leuven: Peeters, 2010), pp. 123–83.

28. Cf. Origen, *Hom. in Jeremiam* 20, Griechischen christlichen Schriftsteller der ersten drei Jahrhunderte [GCS] 6:176–77); Tertullian, *Contra Marcionem* 2.23–24 (SC 368:136–42).

29. Cf. Cyprian, *De invidia et livore* 5 (CCSL 3a:77); Basil, *Hom. de invidia* 3 (PG 31:376c–d).

30. *Hom. de Davide et Saule* 1.1 (PG 54:677); ibid. 1.2 (PG 54:679); ibid. 1.3–4 (PG 54:680–81).

to stand, Chrysostom still discerns signs of remorse, perhaps even repentance, in Saul's final days.[31] But the interpretive consensus was that Saul made his own tragic bed. As Aphrahat the Persian concluded, quoting 1 Thessalonians 5:19, Saul "quenched the Spirit" and didn't look back.[32]

Clearly these biblical tragedies exhibited a wide array of tragic features and themes, but there were consistent interpretive challenges to modulate appearances of divine injustice, to amplify reversals of fortune and resultant suffering, to navigate questions of freedom and fate, and to manage audience perceptions and emotions. In the case of Job, who underwent the most devastating reversal of fortune in the entire Old Testament, in a wager no less between God and Satan, these challenges were so enormous that many patristic interpreters chose to treat the story simply as the testing of a saint or moral hero. Their absolute devotion to divine providence kept many of them from conceding that Job's story is actually a monumental assault on traditional theodicies rooted in the Hebrew scriptures. Still, it was reminiscent of ancient tragic heroes victimized by the caprice of the gods. Theodore of Mopsuestia, the prolific fifth-century preacher and commentator, considered the author of Job a perverse tragedian and the book itself as unworthy of the Christian canon of Scripture (though he received conciliar condemnation for doing so).[33] But this was hardly the general view. John Chrysostom's sermons on Job focus on Job's endurance amid testing, hearing out Job's impious and fatalistic outcries but deeming them paradoxical evidence of his deeper faith, especially since Job discounted his wife's even more fatal-

---

31. Ibid. 3.5–6 (PG 54:702–3); ibid. 3.7 (704–5); ibid. 3.8–9 (706–7).
32. *Demonstratio* 6.16 (Patrologia Syriaca 1:297–300).
33. Theodore of Mopsuestia, *Comm. in* Jobum, fragments in *Acta Conciliorum Oecumenicorum*, 4/1: *Concilium universale Constantinopolitanum sub Iustiniano habitum* (Berlin: Walter de Gruyter, 1971), pp. 66–68.

istic counsel to "curse God and die" (Job 2:9). The real tragedy of the book is the three friends' secret envy of Job, their jaded platitudes and rationalizations of his suffering, and their epic failure of compassion.[34] But an anonymous sermon ascribed to Chrysostom presses the tragic pathos of Job's story much further, depicting Job as mulling over his dead children's scattered body parts, trying in vain to reorganize them. Pseudo-Chrysostom thus confesses to his audience, "I am confused in my soul. I think you experience the same as well. How to describe such a great tragedy I do not know, even if I had the most perfect encomium [for Job] on my tongue."[35]

Tragedy in the New Testament

Let us move over into the New Testament, where, in the Gospel of Matthew, we must recall the mass murder of the Holy Innocents, the horror of which was showcased in an entire tradition of patristic sermons and hymns. In my earlier lecture, I quoted a long passage from Basil of Seleucia's sermon for the Feast of the Holy Innocents that did nothing to moderate the spectacular character of the event. The story was hardly bereft of questions of divine providence and justice, given the appearance that the infant Jesus had escaped the slaughter at other babies' expense. One reason for the rise of the Christian Feast of the Holy Innocents was precisely to counteract such criticism, and to expose Christian audiences to the infants' tragic end for purposes of penitence and lamentation. Romanos the Melodist's kontakion *On the Massacre of the Holy Innocents* plays up the graphic horror of the executions, depicting Herod as a war crim-

---

34. *Expositio in Jobum* 2.10 (SC 346:178–82); ibid. 2.9–14 (pp. 174–90).
35. Pseudo-Chrysostom, *Hom. in Job* 1, quoted by Doerfler, *Jephthah's Daughter, Sarah's Son*, pp. 154–55.

inal and infanticidal maniac, against whom the whole creation rose up in indignation.[36] Other preachers, like John Chrysostom and Peter Chrysologus, sought to divert to a happier ending, namely, the glorious martyrdom to which the infant boys were totally passive and thereby totally exemplary.[37] As Gregory Nazianzen put it, they were "sacrificed before the New Victim [i.e., Jesus Christ],"[38] such that we can see an emerging consensus that the massacre bespeaks the turbulent transition as the old dispensation was giving way to the new, and the violence of the Hebrew and Jewish past was giving way to the slowly emerging peace of Christ. As I said in my earlier lecture, there was a risk here too of scaring off the audience in the liturgical celebration, eliciting raw fear more than mercy or empathy. The desired benefit, on the other hand, was to enable the audience to realize, penitently, that they were still living, even after Christ, in the aftermath of this transition, and that they desperately needed to identify with the anguish of their forbears in sacred history.

Two other characters in the New Testament took up their own very different and compelling roles in the tragic drama of this transition and upheaval in the economy of salvation, and were treated by early Christian interpreters as distinctive tragic types: John the Baptist and Judas Iscariot. The Baptist's tragic persona was subtle but significant. Here was a man seemingly predestined to "decrease" (John 3:30), to be eclipsed, to fade; and he is never mentioned in the New Testament after the Gospels save briefly in Acts (1:5, 22). What troubled patristic expositors was that John seemed at times to be in over his head. Twice early on he claims not to know Jesus, the one to whom he was

---

36. *On the Holy Innocents*, Prooemium and strophes 1–17 (SC 110:204–24).
37. Cf. John Chrysostom, *Hom. in Matthaeum* 9.3 (PG 57:179); Peter Chrysologus, *Hom.* 153.2 (CCSL 24b:956–57).
38. *Or.* 38.18 (SC 358:144–46).

enjoined to witness. How could this be, asks Augustine, if John recognized Jesus as the one who should be baptizing *him* (Matt. 3:14)? Theodore of Mopsuestia explained this in terms of a special providence by which John had lived well away from Jesus in the wilderness so that eventual critics could not claim that John's favorable testimony to Jesus was just a function their being blood relatives (Luke 1:36).[39]

John's alleged ignorance might seem innocent enough were it not for the later episode from prison where he sent his disciples to ask Jesus, "Are you he who is to come, or shall we look for another?" (Matt. 11:2–3; Luke 7:19). The scene here is one of great pathos. Was John waffling at the last moment? Both Augustine and John Chrysostom in their sermons put hard rhetorical questions to the Baptist. "Were all your declarations a fraud, a mere stage play and fable?" asks Chrysostom.[40] But he and other patristic preachers exonerated John by arguing that John's question for Jesus was meant solely for the benefit of John's own disciples, in the expectation that Jesus himself would confirm to John's disciples that he, not John, was messiah.[41]

John's confirmed innocence and faithfulness, however, made his terrible demise in the Herodian court appear all the more tragic. Increasingly in the early church, John was interpreted as a proto-Christian ascetical titan because of his defiance of the worldly powers arrayed against Christ. Some preachers suggested that John's last days unfolded like a stage play. Peter Chrysologus, in particular, used tragic ekphrasis to describe Herod's birthday party, at which the young vixen danced for the head of

---

39. For the relevant passage, see Marco Conti, ed. and trans., *Theodore of Mopsuestia: Commentary on John*, Ancient Christian Texts (Downers Grove, IL: IVP Academic, 2010), p. 21 (on John 1:31).
40. *Hom. in Matthaeum* 36.1 (PG 57:413).
41. Cf. John Chrysostom, *Hom. in Matthaeum* 36.1-2 (PG 57:413-14); Peter Chrysologus, *Sermo* 179.2 (CCSL 24b:1086).

the Baptist (Matt. 14:6–12): "A house is transformed into an arena, the table turns into a theater, dinner guests become spectators, a banquet is turned into frenzy, a meal becomes carnage, wine changes to blood, a funeral is held on a birthday [of Herod], to mark one person's beginning is another person's ending, a banquet morphs into a murder scene, musical instruments ring out a tragedy for the ages (*tragoediam saeculorum*)."⁴² Peter went further and toyed with the idea that this tragedy was also a very dark comedy, a showcase of fools. His Eastern contemporary, Hesychius of Jerusalem, agreed, but also suggested that John got the last laugh, since his prophetic invective is what outed the utter profligacy of the Herodian court.⁴³

In the West, however, both Hilary of Poitiers and Augustine further projected that the tragedy of John the Baptist, similar to that of the Holy Innocents, was a consequence of his liminality, being caught as a tragic protagonist in the middle of a critical flashpoint in sacred history. Jesus himself had announced that the violence accompanying the arrival of his eschatological Kingdom had erupted beginning with John the Baptist (Matt. 11:11–12; Luke 16:16). Hilary calls John the climax of the prophetic tradition,⁴⁴ while Augustine calls him the very boundary (*limes*) between Old and New Testaments,⁴⁵ and Basil of Seleucia deems him the very consummation of the Law (along with Christ), a mediator (*mesitês* / μεσίτης) of old and new covenants alike.⁴⁶

The downfall of Judas Iscariot might seem to present a fairly simple contrast with that of John the Baptist, given Judas's legendary villainy in the historical Christian imagination. But

---

42. *Serm.* 127.9 (CCSL 24b:786), trans. William Palardy, Fathers of the Church 110:190 (slightly altered).
43. *Hom.* 24, Greek text ed. Michel Aubineau, *Les homélies festales d'Hésychius de Jérusalem*, 2 vols. (Brussels: Société des Bollandists, 1980), 2:698.
44. *Comm. in Matthaeum* 14.7–8 (SC 258:16–20).
45. *Sermo* 293.2 (PL 38:1328).
46. *Hom.* 18.2 (PG 85:229c).

there were disturbing questions even in Judas's case. Was Judas, somewhat like Jephthah in the Old Testament, someone who meant well, committing to Jesus' circle of disciples (Mark 3:19 *et par.*), only to be undone by a tragic flaw or miscalculation? Was he a dupe overwhelmed by Satan's bid to possess him (John 13:27; cf. 6:70–71)? If he was a born loser, ever a villain in the making, why did Jesus choose him as a disciple in the first place? In retrospect, Jesus' statement that it were better for the one who betrays him not to have been born (Mark 14:21 *et par.*) sounds pretty fateful.

As in so many biblical tragedies I have been analyzing in patristic interpretation, there was often a veil, however thin, between determinism and freedom, not as abstractions but as arising from the moral dynamics of concrete situations. The second-century Gnostic *Gospel of Judas* made Judas into a hero who was actually predestined to aid Jesus in being delivered from his incarnation, such that the other disciples were the truly tragic figures, being predestined *not* to understand Jesus' true, spiritual rather than fleshly, identity.[47] Origen could not have disagreed more. While conceding that Judas came under Satan's sway, Judas had enjoyed free will from the outset, such that in the end, he even showed an inkling of remorse when he handed the blood money back over to the Temple officials.[48] Origen, Chrysostom, and others in turn conceded a certain benevolent "necessity" in Judas's role in the divine economy: his handing over of Jesus providentially being allowed to serve the Father's handing over of the Son for his salvific passion and death. But Augustine went further: God predestined Judas to be a "son of

---

47. For the text, see Simon Gathercole, trans., *The Gospel of Judas: Rewriting Early Christianity* (New York: Oxford University Press, 2007).
48. *Comm. in Matthaeum* (Latin series) 117 (GCS38:243–50); *Contra Celsum* 2.11 (SC 132:312).

perdition";[49] and every bit as severe was Hilary's claim that as Jesus succumbed to death on the cross, he let out one last anguished gasp because he had been able to cover the sins of all human beings *except Judas's*.[50] Over time, early Christian liturgy increasingly addressed the full tragedy of Judas's betrayal. Chrysostom devoted two entire homilies to the betrayal in order to stir his audiences to godly fear before approaching the Eucharist. Romanos's kontakion on Judas for Holy Thursday introduced new dialogue and new indictments to the story in order to integrate audiences into the action and to elicit fear, outrage, lament, repentance, and their own cries for divine mercy.

Conclusion

Let me conclude this lecture with some parting reflections on the potential benefits for contemporary homiletics and homilists that can be retrieved from patristic expositions of biblical tragedy. I should first mention the fact that the very genre of tragedy as having literary, philosophical, or theological value for Christianity has been the subject of lively recent debate. Already, in the early 1960s, the esteemed literary critic George Steiner argued that Christianity, with its hopeful eschatology, bid for transcendence, and resistance to despair, inaugurated the demise of classical tragedy. Christianity, he claimed, was *essentially* antitragic.[51] For different reasons, some contemporary Christian theologians have also judged tragedy and Christianity incompatible. David Bentley Hart of late has argued that classical tragedy is too pathos-laden, too morally jumbled, and

---

49. *Tractatus in Johannem* 107.7 (CCSL 36:615); cf. *Enarrationes in Psalmos* 108 (CCSL 40:1585–601).
50. *Comm. in Matthaeum* 33.6 (SC 258:254–56).
51. *The Death of Tragedy* (New York: Alfred A. Knopf, 1961).

too thematically diffuse to serve Christian theological ends.[52] The English theologian John Milbank shows a similar aversion to tragic mimetics in Christian theology, lest a tragic worldview take on a life of its own in Christian thinking.[53]

Other theologians have charged ahead, none more prolifically than the late Hans Urs von Balthasar, in his famous series on *Theo-Drama*, which dared to present Christ himself as a particular kind of tragic hero, insofar as, by his incarnation, he plumbed the experiential depths of abandonment by God.[54] The British theologian Donald MacKinnon, along with Paul Janz and Rowan Williams whom he has greatly influenced, have insisted that, for theological credibility's sake, Christianity must engage the "intractably" tragic in this world, suffering that defies resolution or any intrinsic moral calculus of compensation. That is, it must deal with suffering of an intransigent kind that seems to defy meaning itself and yet presses us toward God rather than toward comprehensive explanations of evil. For these Christian thinkers, classical Greco-Roman tragedy has undoubtedly provided a rich resource for exploring the intractably tragic.[55]

---

52. See his "The Gospel according to Melpomene: Reflections on Rowan Williams' *The Tragic Imagination*," *Modern Theology* 34 (2018): 220–34.
53. John Milbank, *The Word Made Strange: Theology, Language, Culture* (Oxford: Blackwell, 1997), pp. 18–24.
54. On tragedy and revelation, see von Balthasar, *The Glory of the Lord: A Theological Aesthetics*, vol. 2, *Studies in Theological Style: Clerical Styles*, trans. Andrew Louth et al. (San Francisco: Ignatius Press, 1984), pp. 31–94 (on Irenaeus of Lyons); and *Theo-Drama: Theological Dramatic Theory*, vol. 2, *Dramatis Personae: Man in God*, trans. Graham Harrison (San Francisco: Ignatius Press, 1990), pp. 37–89; also *Theo-Drama*, vol. 5, *The Last Act*, trans. Graham Harrison (San Francisco: Ignatius Press, 1998), pp. 191–246. For analysis, see also Blowers, *Visions and Faces of the Tragic*, pp. 223–36.
55. Cf. Donald MacKinnon, *The Problem of Metaphysics* (Cambridge: Cambridge University Press, 1974), pp. 122–35; MacKinnon, "Atonement and Tragedy," in his *The Borderlands of Theology and Other Essays* (London: Lutterworth Press, 1968), pp. 97–104; Paul Janz, *God, the Mind's Desire: Reference, Reason, and Christian Thinking* (Cambridge: Cambridge University Press, 2004); Rowan Williams, *The Tragic Imagination* (Oxford: Oxford University Press, 2016).

For their part, the early Christian preachers and interpreters that I have been referencing were less interested in whether, in strictly theoretical or artistic terms, biblical narratives could qualify as "tragic" by classical pagan standards than in treating biblical tragedies on their own terms, albeit allowing thematic overlap with the classical tragedies on matters of divine justice and providence, human freedom, the multiformity of evil, and the putative power of fate. Though we have seen their attempts to squeeze meaning out of seemingly irredeemable stories like that of Jephthah's vow, and to obviate moral dead-ends and appearances of determinism, there is still a healthy resistance to viewing biblical tragedy through rose-colored glasses. Exemplary for preachers today is the early interpreters' refusal to erase the intransigence of tragedy and let go Scripture's ability to tease Christians' moral imagination in order to form it. Though these ancient expositors were committed to traditional teaching about divine providence and sovereignty, they fully understood that there is no systematic theodicy in the Bible, any more than there is a monochrome theory of evil. They let the fierce realism of tragic narratives and characters have its say, as it were, and allowed Christians to envision a world devoid of providence and justice as the paradoxical basis for maturing their faith therein.

Another benefit for contemporary homiletics to be retrieved from early Christian exposition of biblical tragedy is the assiduous rhetorical exercise of modulating *but also retraining* an audience's emotional responses to tragic circumstances in Scripture, and, by extension, tragedy in Christians' experiential foreground. Many patristic expositors knew of Aristotle's designation of fear and pity as the normative tragic emotions demanding catharsis or "cleansing." Some classicists believe that Aristotle intended this catharsis to be more than just a ventilation of pent-up emotion in the face of human suffering. Be that as it may, Christian preachers and hymnists looked meticulously to reeducate emotions that would give dimension to faith. Early in book 3 of his *Confessions*, Augustine reminisces on how in Carthage he used to watch tragic plays in the amphitheater and bawl his eyes out with "tragic pity" for the characters; but then he castigates himself for having succumbed to the sick pleasure of emotional voyeurism, expending false pity on false characters' false suffering. However, at least this might serve as a practice run for feeling authentic mercy and compassion for those in the real world who suffer in all sorts of ways, especially those who revel in their own debauchery.[56] So, too, the patristic expositors of biblical tragedy, aware of Plato's famous criticism of the tragedians as traffickers in raw emotion, remained acutely conscious of how quickly even decent emotions could go awry and take on a life of their own. Romanos the Melodist, for example, knew full well that his *Kontakion on Judas* could potentially lead its listeners in errant directions, toward an overload of horror and revulsion, or even an impious schadenfreude, rather than penitent identification with the spiritually bereft soul of Judas. The live preacher, more than the poet, however, at least had the advantage of scouting his audience's emotions in the midst of liturgical observances and in the contexts of pastoral care. The hymnist like Romanos had no such ability directly to monitor or calibrate the emotions of those who heard his kontakia sung in worship.

Finally, one of the greatest legacies of patristic preaching on biblical tragedy for contemporary homilists, I suggest, was its effectiveness in refining Christian hope, all the more so against the backdrop of a Roman moral and philosophical culture in which hope had never achieved status as a virtue and was largely considered a dangerous form of wishful thinking or self-delusion. The British literary critic and occasional Catholic philosopher-

---

56. *Confessiones* 3.2.3–4 (CCSL 27:28–29).

theologian Terry Eagleton, whose book *Hope without Optimism* tracks various developments in Christian hope historically, observes that the key for Christianity has been to navigate its hope between the extremes of despair, on the one hand, and simplistically pious triumphalism on the other.[57] Early Christian preachers were already doing just that, averting both a collapse into desperation and a naïve grab after transcendence. As we see in the sermon of Pseudo-Chrysostom on Job that I briefly mentioned earlier, Christians were called to sit with Job on the pile of his children's scattered body parts if they were to have any hope of discerning God's ultimate mercy. Only by imaginatively visiting the existential cul-de-sac where evil's caprice seemed to rule the day could the serious Christian empathize with the despairing masses. All the while, the crucial factor for refining and focusing Christian hope was the recognition of God's condescension, through Jesus Christ, into the abyss where human beings aspire, with or without hope, to make sense of the world they inhabit, a world all at once horrifying and beautiful. No doubt this is one reason that patristic commentators were so drawn to Paul's vision, in Romans 8, of God's provisional subjection of the world to vanity, to a dialectic of flourishing and languishing, which was nonetheless an act of grace, since, as Paul further asserts, it is a subjection *in hope* (8:20, 24–25). Tragedies in the Bible, as these ancient interpreters perceived, simply dramatized and intensified what Paul described as the groaning of the whole creation in anticipation of its transformation (8:22–23). Solidarity in hope meant trusting patiently and soberly with other Christians in the freedom of God still to act in a world where tragedy and new creation seem mysteriously intertangled. As Augustine among others insisted, genuine hope does not just

---

57. *Hope without Optimism* (Charlottesville: University of Virginia Press, 2015), esp. pp. 39–89.

launch out on its own; it is invariably anchored in the other "theological virtues" of faith and love (1 Cor. 13:13). But the additional (albeit counterintuitive) message of patristic preachers on biblical tragedy for contemporary homilists, is that hope itself must find its place alongside fear, mercy, grief, and lamentation (etc.) as part of a uniquely Christian tragic pathos, the full repertoire of emotions befitting Christians, who both recognize the incalculable evil infesting human existence and doggedly envision the Creator overthrowing it.

AUTHOR-AUDIENCE DISCUSSION

AUDIENCE MEMBER: The question that's always fascinated me in my academic work is "post-Enlightenment," this division that seems to have arisen even in Christian circles, especially among academics who study the scholastics, between "reason" and "feeling." And it seems that the Fathers offer a really wonderful response to that so we can get back to more integrated, holistic experience as Christians. Would you speak to that a bit?

PAUL BLOWERS: That's great! I think one thing that early Christian writers and intellectuals gleaned from classical moral philosophy, particularly from the Platonic tradition, but even from Stoic tradition, was a very healthy moral psychology, the sense that, particularly in play, was a Platonic model, an anthropological model, where reason negotiates between the higher spirit or mind and the lower soul and its proclivities for passions, particularly the desiring faculty and the thematic or faculty of temper or anger. Reason disciplines and navigates the emotions. Reason can't get away from the higher calling of the spirit (*nous* / νοῦς). Neither can it just escape from the lower faculties of desire and aversion because it needs them all. And this is one of the things, I think, that becomes intrinsic to much of early Christian virtue ethics: the sense that we don't just act on pure reason. We're not Kantians, after all, and we don't act by any sort of pure moral power of reasoning. We are a complex set of faculties that the *nous* is trying to rally, the mind is trying to rally and bring order to. Of course, one take on the Fall is that it threw all this into chaos, and asceticism—which is the calling of all Christians, and not just monastics—has to reorder that. Nobody's going to accuse these writers of being rationalists, and no one's going to accuse them of being emotionalists. And there's a clear recognition of the complexity of the human self. This is why Augustine, as Rowan Williams said in his 2023 lecture, Augustine is so compelling because he knows this tradition and he's lived it. So, it takes on a different kind of aura. The only other person in antiquity that bears their soul as much as Augustine in a literary way is Gregory Nazianzen in his autobiographical poetry. He *totally* bears his soul. These are people who are philosophically gifted. They know the rules of logic and rhetoric and philosophy, and yet they also know that we are complex beings and that our *pathai* (πάθαι), our emotions, are a vital part of it all. Pathos in Greek is a very tricky term, because it can mean a lot of different things, and typically *pathai* gets translated "passions," but they're also what the Stoics called, the *eupatheiai* (εὐπάθειαι), "the good, the useful, the valuable emotions." We could almost say "reasonable emotions." And so all of those things are supposed to play together. And I think one of the things that's powerful about these authors who are dealing with tragedy is they are recognizing that we are a step away from dissolving into utter chaos. That's Augustine's point, right? We're always on the brink, and we're always needing to be reordered. We're always needing to be called back. And these stories, these tragic stories, push us to think all these kinds of things through. They do today what maybe we would call theologically-geared psychoanalysis of biblical characters. They are definitely interested in their interior lives.

AUDIENCE MEMBER: As you were speaking, I couldn't help but think of Gregory the Great. I don't know if there was a lot of theater going on in Rome and his time because of the Lombards on one side, and God knows what else, everywhere else. And he was just trying to keep things together. He was educated and he was a smart cookie. But one of his books that meant a lot to me, and so much so that I gave it away to a bunch of pastors, is his book on pastoral psychology, his "pastoral rule." I'd read that, and I'd think, "Who was this guy?" I mean, eat your heart out, Sigmund Freud. Gregory the Great was thinking about this stuff. And what was interesting to me was things like, "How do you talk to somebody who talks all the time?" I'm using a lighter example. "How do you talk to somebody who won't talk at all?" And then he delves into this, the psyche, if you will, of the people. And just as you were talking, I couldn't help but think of him writing that into a world that was a mess, as is our own, and desperate stuff going on around Rome. But I don't know if the theater was there or not.

PAUL BLOWERS: At that point in time, theater—stage theater — was certainly in decline. It took a long time, of course, for tragic stage plays completely to die out and comedies and so on. But your point's an important one. That treatise, of course, became the model for medieval pastoral care. Interestingly, it's built on Gregory Nazianzen in his second oration, where he had left the ministry and said, "I can't handle this. I'm going off to my ascetic retreat." And then he comes back to town with his tail between his legs and gets up in front of the audience and reads off this incredible oration describing the high calling of pastoral care and going into all this detail about how you possibly accommodate the gospel to all these people of so many different types. And that's where Gregory the Great picks up on it. He also is picking up on John Chrysostom's treatise on the priesthood, which does a lot of the same things. The thing that's beautiful about those texts is it's moral psychology at its best. They're exploring how we're outfitted, not only for vice but for virtue, and how everything is an aesthetical struggle that's known by everyone. And that certainly broke some very important ground particularly, again, in the Middle Ages, for pastoral care, especially by the time you get to the later Middle Ages and pastoral care is broken down significantly in the Western churches.

AUDIENCE MEMBER: It was the standard text, practically, for pastoral service up until the Renaissance and Baroque period, until others started writing more compendious discussions. But it was translated into Anglo-Saxon and was translated by Chaucer. It was *"the* book," if a priest had a book that was professional manual, apart from the scriptures or the office, he had it. Yeah, very important.

AUDIENCE MEMBER: In what sense could tragedy function as what Paul talks about in the sixth chapter of Ephesians, when he refers to "principalities and powers"? With political tragedies, there's suffering, war is there, as well. Is there some sense in which that can morph into something that would approximate what Paul calls "principalities and powers."

PAUL BLOWERS: First of all, one of the things, I think, that attracted early Christian writers to at least some aspects of Greco-Roman tragedy was the abiding influence of this sense that was deeply built into the pagan psyche, that we are ruled by forces that are out of our control. Paul talks in Galatians and elsewhere about "the elements," the elemental forces; there are things that are just out of our control, that we don't have any direct control over. Christ rules, but it's still a battle. And again, Greco-Roman tragedy loved to think in terms of these kinds of forces, and how we are sucked into the black hole of circumstances where we don't even know what we're going to hang on to. The interesting thing is, how do you balance that with the confidence of the Christian hope? I think Paul probably does it as well as anybody in Romans 8. We're subjected to vanity and hope. We're in this weird dialectic in this life between flourishing and languishing, and we keep going back, and we're being undermined, and we're undermining ourselves. But there's also the human experience that we're undermined—by the elements, the physical elements. We're destabilized all the time by governments, by the weather, you name it, it's still there. There's still a cosmic battle going on. Christianity has never ultimately conceded to a dualistic cosmology, where it's God versus all the forces of evil in the cosmos that are arrayed against him. There's more interest in the sort of the moral battle against God and the powers that be. But I think again, that's where a sort of tragic perspective retains value.

I was speaking earlier about this notion of the "intractably tragic events," the sense that there's certain things that happen to people that they'll never be compensated for in this life. And it's not in the best interest of the church to say, well, "You got a home in gloryland that outshines the sun." And just to go there mentally. Tragedy provides us a way to deal with the intractably tragic. I love Rowan Williams's point in his little book on tragedy, which came out a few years ago, which is excellent. He says, the intractably tragic is where people experience certain things that just have no moral calculus of compensation built into the system. You know, philosophers like Aristotle could talk all day about distributive justice, and in the best of all possible worlds, everybody's going to get what they deserve. Well, we know what Job does with the Deuteronomic historian's idea that "everybody's going to get what they deserve." We need complexity. We need exposure to chaos in order to reorder our faith, and that is a hard, hard battle. Anybody who's done pastoral care with people who are just engulfed in intense bereavement, like those parents in Aberfan, Wales, in 1966 pulling their kids out of coal sludge and burying them; we have to grapple with it. We don't have any choice if we want any credibility as the church.

AUDIENCE MEMBER: I am thinking of that occasion where Jesus talks about how these people were in a tower somewhere, and it fell, and how they were not any more sinful than somebody else. And right there, that's the Son of God saying, "No, they weren't." That one always brings me up short when I read that passage. Because, OK, the fact that I don't like it when my father died is big to me, but small stuff.

PAUL BLOWERS: This reminds me of Rowan Williams's point about this notion of moral calculus. Remember the text about Lazarus we discussed this morning, where John Chrysostom says that Lazarus is emitting all this grievance about how unfairly he's been treated, and everybody else is luxuriating. But we're all going to be morally leveled one way or the other, right? We're all going to be brought to ground zero. I think that's what judgment is, in a sense. And, yeah, I think whenever we begin to think of providence and justice and these kinds of things in terms of a calculus, we get ourselves into real problems. So, it's funny to me still how easily the prosperity gospel can kind of trickle into Christian discourse and rhetoric, in very subtle kinds of ways that are not helpful at all.

AUDIENCE MEMBER: In putting your presentation together. I'm wondering what your process was, because almost in every biblical story, there's an element of tragedy, sometimes "happy endings," and sometimes, like you said, the existential dead-end. Where would Jonah fit into this as he is being thrown into the seas, ecumenically, by people of different faiths and him agreeing to go. "Yeah, you're right. I screwed up with my God." But there's a "happy ending" because he does what he's supposed to do at the end. So, walk us through which ones you picked. Are there other characters that didn't make the cut?

PAUL BLOWERS: Yes, of course. A lot of Old Testament scholars think Jonah is a comedy, not a tragedy. Seriously, that it's a piece of biblical comedy. All the ironies you know, Jonah seems so pious. You read that prayer, his penitential prayer in chapter 2, just such a beautiful psalmlike text, but the story ends with him feeling sorry for himself, sulking under a plant. Jonah ponders the ironies of God's justice, the utter irony of God showing grace to the Ninevites "who don't know their right hand from their left," and all that kind of stuff. So the story is often seen as comedy. Now in my book on all this I deal with what we sometimes call "tragic comedy," or "tragicomedy," as Shakespeare called it, where the two are mixed together. For example, the story of Jacob and Esau. Sibling rivalries are always very interesting because there's a lot of sibling rivalry in tragic literature like sons of Oedipus who end up killing each other. But the story of Jacob and Esau, if you look at it superficially, is hilarious. Here's Jacob, the mama's boy. Rachel favors Jacob. Here's Esau that gives away his birthright for a bowl of lentils. Even some ancient writers recognized that this is actually pretty funny, what he gave away for a bowl of lentils. And this is not to mention the way in which Jacob just turns out to be this compromised character, this young man shrewd-from-the-womb. He's a kind of a huckster, and yet he ends up thriving, and he gets the legacy of carrying all the Abrahamic tradition. But here's what makes it a "comedy" on Aristotle's terms: it has a happy ending because the brothers don't kill each other, they reconcile. It's a long story. It's long and it's developed. At the end of the day, they reconcile and ostensibly live happily ever after. Samson is sometimes considered to be a tragic character. His story is just so weird. And see who else in the New Testament. I didn't mention Ananias and Sapphira in Acts, who pay dearly for holding back from the giving of goods to the community, and they pay dearly by their deaths. There's a famous pagan critic of Christianity, Porphyry of Tyre, who had studied the Bible and who was a famous critic of Scripture known by Christian writers including Augustine. Porphyry's take is that Peter and the church overreacted. I mean, really, Peter, who denied Christ, isn't that a heck of a lot more horrible a crime to commit than putting a little bit back in your IRA. A Christian apologist, a guy named Macarius Magnus, who almost nobody knows anything about, answered that critique, and just basically said, "As you would expect, they got exactly what they deserved because they quenched the Spirit." They blasphemed, they made a promise to God and broke it. And it usually doesn't work out well for you when that happens, you know.

So, when I was writing on this stuff I was looking for everything I could find. And I know that I didn't cover all the bases.

There are too many narratives that would have to be treated. I was more interested in the ones where you wouldn't necessarily, superficially say this is "tragic," like John the Baptist. He's a really interesting character, and there's some real disturbing things there. He was getting himself into something he wasn't completely comprehending. So, remember these people are facing the fact too, that there are tensions within the Bible and how things are presented. They're dealing with that, and they're trying to reconcile things, and they're trying to, in a sense, be fair to the complexity of figures and stories but also provide some path forward toward coherence. And there are dangers. We talked about them this morning. Sometimes the preacher maybe overreaches a little bit in the direction of trying to provide a "happily ever after." But again, I still sympathize with the cause and I totally side with folks like Rowan Williams, Paul Jantz, and also Ben Quash, who's supposed to be in this lecture series. I think he's another who thinks we can't do without this kind of—what they will call—"the tragic vision of things," tragic vision of life.

AUDIENCE MEMBER: When you were speaking, I thought about the beginning of *Mere Christianity* by Lewis. He asks, have you ever felt like something wasn't fair? Children have this innate sense of fairness that you don't have to teach them that something isn't right, or that they deserve *x* or whatever. And he says, oh, well, that's because that's the heart of God, that's judgment and fairness. That's where you get it. So, we innately have this sense of right and wrong. And then, as you're speaking, I thought, well, of course, there's tragedy in the Bible. It's like poop hitting the fan the whole way through. Almost no one has redemption. Samson's mother prays and prays and prays and her son's a train wreck, like it's not great. For those making the pro/con arguments about tragedy in the Bible, what are they arguing? Are they arguing, yes, there's tragedy, but you know who wins in the end, so there's really not tragedy? Or, there's tragedy in it, but Jesus didn't gnash his teeth, so you really shouldn't be tragic, like he just wept, so you can weep and move on? What's their big claim either way? Because I believe that the human condition is tragic, and we know who wins in the end, but it doesn't dismiss the tragedy of the human existence. I mean, Jesus is overwhelmed. He comes to the earth and he's overwhelmed. He sees all this tragedy, and I don't know, I'm just confused how someone wouldn't think that there's tragedy.

PAUL BLOWERS: I think the important thing to remember relates to the sort of refining of hope that I talked about. These writers are on to the fact that diverting to a happy ending in the eschatological end, a sort of final reckoning and retribution and so on, is not going to speak well in the moment. It would be like going to the funeral of all those little kids in Wales, and the pastor is saying, "Folks, just hang in there. Your grief will let up over time, and there's a great ending coming." All of us who've done funerals know what it's like, the temptation to say you will see your loved one again, and so forth and so on. But I think good parents need to train up their kids early on to see this point, that there isn't this built-in moral calculus. We need fairness. We obviously need a certain sense of justice. But even in our national conversations now about justice and equity, the whole thing has become really sloppy, and some are constantly calling for real material equity. Is that possible? If it's not possible, let's find other ways to navigate this discussion, and we're not very good at that yet, but it goes back to the struggles we face in helping children and grandchildren know what it means to face the world and to be there, beholding its tragedies. The kid I sat next to in junior high band murdered his mother. I talked to him one day, and the next day, he went and stabbed his mother to death. It absolutely disturbed my worldview, needless to say, and it's hard because you also don't want to project the sense that the world is just horrifically fearful, and that you should live in constant anxiety. Obviously, that's not healthy either. But moral formation is something vitally important within the home, within the school. This is why we have so many private schools now, saying, if kids can't get morally formed in a public setting, we're going to have to take matters into our own hands. Church has the truly formative role, the role of liturgy, the role of catechesis. I come from a tradition that doesn't have a catechumenate, but we did have being drilled into us from day one, learning the scriptures and memorizing them and having them internalized in our souls, in ways that that did inoculate us to a certain degree. When I was in fifth grade, and we went on a youth group outing to a swimming pool, one of the kids in our group drowned. They pulled him out and laid him beside the pool. We stood there breathless, and yet immediately after that happened, our youth group leaders worked with us to help us to begin the process of trying to manage our grief. That's what this can look like. One of the things about these writers I've been talking about is that they paid incredible attention to emotional formation. Look at Augustine. His analysis of human desire, his analysis of grief, his analysis of mercy. A lot of it is out of his own formation and experience and struggle and so forth. But these people pay close attention to our emotional life and how we're constantly having to navigate it. So, yes, your question is huge.

AUDIENCE MEMBER: I'm really grateful for the depth and evocative nature of this second talk, and for pointing us to the reality of tragedy. You mentioned Job and the Fathers talking about the envy and the failure of his friends. What always strikes me is they sit with him for a week, just mourning with him before they open their mouths. And that is so hard to do. It is so hard to sit in the presence of grief and just be, and it strikes me that this talk reminds us that it's essential. As you said earlier, we live in a world where we are still at war against the forces of evil. Satan still is the prince of this world. And you look at the kind of agony of suffering that's happening in Palestine, and it rips your heart out. But what can you do but pray, or you think about what's happening in Sudan. It's not just war, but it's also famine. So I think this is just such a timely reminder of the need for us as Christians to deal with tragedy and the inexplicable nature of it.

And I also had a question from your earlier talk, which I thought would have been appropriate here, because you said you were going to talk about modern homiletics. I just wondered, if you know about Michael Todd, who is a pastor, I believe, in Memphis, you talked about theatrics. He rarely uses theatrics in the way you describe. He literally sits in a boat in water on the stage when, for example, doing a sermon about Jesus and the disciples going out on the lake, or something like that.

PAUL BLOWERS: Good for him!

AUDIENCE MEMBER: Well, that's my question. Is it really good? Because I wonder, at what point do we cross from bringing insight into the Scripture and into the lessons in Scripture, into simply *entertaining*? Because I don't know what people learn, what more they learn, because he's sitting in a boat on the stage. And I would love to hear you comment on that, but I'd add one

PATRISTIC PREACHING   71

other thing. You mentioned, the "dangers of theatrics." Michael Todd encountered this firsthand. In some sermon to illustrate his point, he spits on his actual brother, and Twitter was just overwhelmed and all the negatives that could possibly arise. But I'm curious, at what point can the theatrics, especially taken to the level at which he is taking them, cross from edification into being counterproductive entertainment?

Paul Blowers: That is a wonderful question, and very timely in terms of how "theatrical preaching" has played out, particularly in American religious history, and so on. It's funny to me, by the way, that always people think that Jonathan Edwards with his famous sermon "Sinners in the Hands of an Angry God," that he was intense, scaring the hell out of everybody. Jonathan Edwards was very sedate. You're a sinner in the hands of the angry God. You will be judged. You know, it's very, very sedate, very rational. George Whitefield, who I was mentioning this morning, was totally different. The more theatrics, the better. And of course, the evangelical traditions have seen plenty of different phases of that and different manifestations of it.

I think part of the issue, though, for homilists and preachers is that you have to have a certain amount of communicative trust with the people that you're preaching to, that they are able to see that you're not just performing a bunch of antics here. You're deadly serious about this. I'm all for thoughtful ways in which to do that. Of course, now you'll go to many of these sort of contemporary Protestant services where there are the big screens, where they'll have a prefabricated video and all kinds of effects, light, and fog to induce the audience. But does that work so well as the subtlety of the aura of incense and candles ? I'm standing here looking at these theater lights right in my face. What a lot of entertaining-type preachers need to do is learn the mastery of subtlety. My wife and I watch a lot of British television, and one reason we do that is because the British are masters of subtlety in underplaying things in a way that will knock your socks off. Americans, they want overplay a lot of the time, and sometimes there's good reason for that. Sometimes there's good reason for much animation. And of course, there are variances according to different traditions and different congregational needs and so forth and so on. But I don't think there are any rules other than that preaching that is using some manner of, or manifestations of artistry, is acutely self-conscious, acutely aware of the power of the scriptural texts themselves. That requires immense self-awareness on the part of the homilist, the preacher. But I think over time, you can cultivate that effectively. For one thing, the longer you preach to the same audience, the more you're familiar with them, the more they trust you. Thus, the more you're able, as I was talking about with some of these ancient preachers, to calibrate their emotions, to get a sense of their emotional temperament, their emotional barometer, knowing as in Gregory the Great when to push, to shove, to move, to pull back, even be silent, the better. There's a lot of dynamics in that knowing. It's just like good actors. They are incredibly self-aware on stage. Any single movement you make can have some sort of effect in the audience. Indeed, quite often the audience isn't even aware that they're being subconsciously affected by these things. But of course, a really fine actor often has a very fine script too, with a playwright who has thought through these things, and so, yes, I'm intensely interested in the dynamics shared between the theater stage and preaching. They don't always sit nicely together, but they can sure learn a lot from each other.

Father Hugh's Opening Remarks to the Lectures

Well, you have before you, in your program a perfectly adequate description of the accomplishments and the qualifications of our speaker today. But one thing which might not occur to you, which is very providential and hopeful for the rest of our day, is that Paul Blowers comes to us on the Feast of the Conversion of St. Paul. So, it's what I call my "liturgical astrology." You know, the conjunctions? I'm always noticing these conjunctions occur more often than you might imagine. Where you have a day planned, and then you realize as you look at the martyrology—there's maybe some of you who don't look at the martyrology every day—"Oh, my goodness, every day is full of possibilities for conjunctions." And so, you just practice that. You know, you get out your "liturgical astrolabe," and figure out just whom to invoke, right? And so, we're very happy to have a professor with us here. I spoke last night with him, not at great length but at some length, and took a measure of the cheerful, learned, and engaged sort of man that he is, and we can expect to receive a portion of all of that.

You know, affect is a very important aspect of any type of communication. And certainly, theatricality is definitely concerned with affect. As priests of this Abbey, there's a really strong emphasis on the speculative tradition, and so studying everything in the light of, and according to the writings of, St. Thomas Aquinas. And then secondarily, even though we follow his rule, the teaching of St. Augustine and the fathers of the church. Well, of course, the principal instrument of the fathers was rhetoric. It was the persuasive form of classical culture, and the principal form for St. Thomas was the speculative form, that of the *questio*, which developed out of the rhetorical tradition. But to be really persuasive, you need to act it out. The proof of this is in our Lord's own institution of his Eucharist, which is, in effect, sacred drama, which is reenacted every single day, Sunday after Sunday throughout the world, so that we might not forget His work of love for us.

Affect and theatricality has everything to do with who we are. It's at the heart of our religion, and sometimes, if we lament the less than engaging or inspiring aspects of Christian worship, it's often because the theatrical element—and I don't mean the self-referential, but the theatrical element, that is, the drama of God's saving work—is not conveyed in a way that is sufficiently complete, something to see, something to hear, some gesture to perform, something to sing, to be surrounded by, as the church always has.

If you think of a great cathedral, a big liturgy, the evensong in an English cathedral, you know, you see the point, it's all there for you. And so, in our hearts today, let's build that context of medi-tation on the holy mysteries of our faith and look for the signs and the evidence of the drama being worked out in each one of our lives. Because, believe me, it's a big drama to struggle with the evil one and our Savior, and we're there in the middle being tugged at from one side and efficaciously moved from the other. And so, let's give thanks and begin our day with great expectation.

Author's Comments and Acknowledgments

I want to thank the Ahmansons and the Fieldstead and Company team and the pure genius of those who conceived this lectureship. I also want to thank the Abbey for hospitality and for beautifully bearing the love of Christ.

I also want to say a word about Henry Chadwick and Tom Oden. For lack of a better term, in my entire career, I've been a "Henry Chadwick groupie." It started when I was just a young scholar, and the first work that I ever read in early Christian studies was Henry Chadwick's translation of Origen's *Contra Celsum*, which is still a monumental work that converted me to the study of early Christianity and the Fathers.

And in later years, I was able to visit with Professor Chadwick a few times, usually at the Oxford Patristic conferences. I went up to him when I was a greenhorn, and he was getting ready to give a talk, and I just told him how much I appreciated him, and told him about my original reading of the translation of the *Contra Celsum*. He could not have been more gracious with me and inspired me and encouraged me, and that's stayed with me. I've read probably just about everything he's ever written, including all of his essays. And yesterday, archivist Thomas Kiser took me into the special collections library here, which for me was like going to Disneyland! And I got to see even some lecture notes of Professor Chadwick. And that was just very deeply moving to me.

Tom Oden, I did know as well, and he was a remarkable individual whose transformation—personally, pastorally, intellectually, over the course of his lifetime—left an incredible legacy. Tom Oden literally opened the door to the study of the ancient Christian tradition to many people whose churches had for centuries ignored it. He spent a week at our seminary several years ago, giving lectures and interacting with faculty and students, and it left a lasting imprint on our community, particularly his passion for the study of patristic pastoral theology.

And so that is an object of great gratitude. And I hope that with what I have to say, I might honor their legacy. As the Orthodox Christians would say, may they be of "memory eternal."

HENRY CHADWICK AND THOMAS C. ODEN

HENRY CHADWICK (1920–2008) was a British theologian and Church of England priest. A leading historian of the early church, Chadwick was appointed Regius Professor at both the universities of Oxford and Cambridge. He was general editor of the Oxford History of the Christian Church, and Oxford Early Christian Texts. His publications included *Origen: Contra Celsum*; *Early Christian Thought and the Classical Tradition*; *Saint Augustine: Confessions* (translation and notes); and *The Early Church* (The Penguin History of the Church).

THOMAS C. ODEN (1931–2016) was an American Methodist theologian, often regarded as the father of the paleo-orthodox theological movement. He was Henry Anson Buttz Professor of Theology at The Theological School, Drew University, and the general editor of the multivolume patristic *Ancient Christian Commentary on Scripture*. The author of numerous books, including a highly regarded three-volume systematic theology, he also served as a general editor for Ancient Christian Texts and as director of the Center for Early African Christianity.

St. Michael's Abbey

Nestled in Southern California's Santiago Canyon, St. Michael's Abbey is regarded as one of the largest communities of the world-wide Norbertine Order. The Abbey's story begins in 1957 when seven Hungarian refugee priests fled from the Communist suppression of their abbey in Csorna, Hungary, and immigrated to Southern California to establish a small monastery in 1961. Today, St. Michael's Abbey has grown to over sixty priests and over forty seminarians in formation. Immersed in a tradition enduring over nine hundred years, the Norbertine Order is named after St. Norbert of Xanten (d. 1134), whose conviction that clerical reform and church renewal were needed in his day through the life and work of monastic communities. St. Augustine of Hippo's rule for clerics, which St. Norbert adopted, continues to be followed among the Norbertines to this day in their communal living and vows of poverty, celibacy, and obedience. St. Michael's Abbey is home to a special collections library that includes papers and fifteen thousand volumes from Henry Chadwick's personal collection, as well as Thomas C. Oden's rare book collection. To learn more about the Abbey, visit stmichaelsabbey.com.

www.ingramcontent.com/pod-product-compliance
Lightning Source LLC
Chambersburg PA
CBHW061810070526
44586CB00024B/2792